FLIP IT!
An Information Skills Strategy for Student Researchers

By Alice H. Yucht

Linworth
PUBLISHING, INC.

PROFESSIONAL
GROWTH
SERIES®

Linworth Publishing, Inc.
Worthington, Ohio

Dedication

This book would not have been possible without the encouragement and nagging of many people, but especially:

- The kids and teachers I've worked with for the past 10 years, who were willing to try out all kinds of new ideas and techniques in an effort to make learning more efficient, effective, and even enjoyable,
- The participants in my workshops, who kept asking for something *in print* to refer back to and share with their peers,
- The fellow school librarians who mentored me, and those whom I now mentor, who understand why lifetime learning skills are our most important contribution to the educational curriculum,
- My husband, fellow librarian and patient listener to my tales and tirades,
- My own two kids, who told me what did and did not work in their own schooling, and why (often in great detail),
- My brother, who showed me how to explore new possibilities,
- And my parents, master-teachers who taught me the importance of asking Why? and What if? and So then what? about everything.

AHY

Library of Congress Cataloging-in-Publication Data

Yucht, Alice H.
    Flip It! an information skills strategy for student researchers / by Alice H. Yucht
       p.   cm. — (Professional growth series)
    Includes bibliographical references (p.)
    ISBN 0-938865-62-5 (perfect bound)
    1. Library orientation for high school students.   2. Library
orientation for middle school students.   3. Information retrieval—
Study and teaching (Secondary)   4. Critical thinking—Study and
teaching (Secondary)   I. Title.   II. Series
Z711.2.Y83   1997   97-3887
025.5678'223—dc21   CIP

Published by Linworth Publishing, Inc.
480 East Wilson Bridge Road, Suite L
Worthington, Ohio 43085

Copyright ©1997 by Linworth Publishing, Inc.

Series Information:

    From the The Professional Growth Series

ISBN 0-938865-62-5

5 4 3 2 1

Table of Contents

Introduction

At Back-To-School night programs I tell parents that the school library is the "Lifetime Learning Skills Lab", where kids learn to be effective information users and knowledge navigators. We explore, investigate, dissect, experiment, and create using the raw materials of fact and fiction to increase our understanding of the world we live in. We try out new models and possibilities for the future while developing our problem-solving skills today. The kids call me Mrs. Y, not just because it's my name, but because that's the question I'm always asking them—Why?— as I help them learn to be curious, creative, and critical thinkers.

FLIP IT! developed because I wanted my students to become self-sufficient information problem-solvers. From its original purpose as a research-skills strategy, it has now become a framework for all kinds of teaching and learning applications, as well as an acronym for a generic problem-solving process. Even the text of this book uses FLIP IT! as an organizing strategy:

Chapter 1, FOCUS, discusses how FLIP IT! evolved, and how the basic elements of learning impact how we teach information literacy skills.

Chapter 2, LINKS, looks at FLIP IT! as an alternate approach to the traditional library skills units, and offers sample lessons and learning activities.

Chapter 3, INPUT, shows how to infuse resource-based learning across the curriculum, demonstrating a variety of ways to revamp traditional "research report" assignments and formats.

Chapter 4, PASSING IT ON, demonstrates ways to help teachers use FLIP IT! as a paradigm for all kinds of educational applications.

As Jamie McKenzie wrote in the March 1997 issue of *From Now On - The Educational Technology Journal* (http://fromnowon.org), ". . . the arrival of new electronic information technologies threatens to overwhelm us with info-glut and info-garbage, . . . (and) schools must make a dramatically expanded commitment to questioning, research, information literacy and student-centered classrooms." Using FLIP IT!, and teaching our students how to use it, can help us develop successful learners, thinkers, and problem-solvers for the next Information Age.

About the Author

Alice H. Yucht has been guiding both children and adults through the mazes of Information Literacy for over 30 years, as a school librarian (K-12, all kinds of schools), a public librarian (YA, children's, reference, and even geriatric services, not necessarily in that order), and an educational consultant. She earned her B.A. in Education/World Cultures at Brooklyn College, and her M.L.S. at Pratt Institute (both in New York City).

For 16 years she's been a middle school librarian, integrating information skills across the curriculum for grades 4 through 8. Her "Filed Above the Rod" column on professional issues has appeared in LIBRARY TALK magazine for the past nine years. She compiled the *Elementary School Librarian's Desk Reference: Library Skills and Management Guide* for Linworth in 1991, and is currently working on the revision of that title. In 1994 she was a member of the selection panel for H.W. Wilson's *Middle/Junior High School Library Collection*, and in 1996 she was the chair of *VOYA* magazine's new NonFiction Honors for Middle School booklist. She is an active member of the Educational Media Association of New Jersey, the American Association of School Librarians, and the Association for Supervision and Curriculum Development, and a frequent poster to LM_NET.

She is also an adjunct instructor at Rutgers University/School of Communication, Information and Library Studies/Professional Development Program, offering courses on Information Skills, Library Management, and Curricular Connections.

Chapter 1

Focus: What FLIP IT! is All About

How FLIP IT! Evolved

For years I watched students stumble through research assignments. Although they usually knew what the final product should be (e.g., the answer to a specific question, a term paper, or a book report), they seemed to have little or no idea how to achieve that result. Too often, I found myself reviewing basic library/information skills and strategies that these students had already learned. With some prompting, they often realized that they did know how to proceed on their own; they just hadn't thought enough about what they should do at each step. What these students needed was an information problem-solving strategy—a process they could learn and use as needed, no matter what the content of the problem they were trying to solve.

Focus: A Generic Research Strategy

In 1988, I had a class of seventh graders who were inquisitive, enthusiastic, and willing to try almost anything new, especially if it wasn't part of the regular curriculum. So I posed the following problem to them: Could we as a team develop a standardized strategy that would help them know what to do on their own in order to solve any kind of informational problem? When I explained that I suspected this kind of strategy might even be a way to help them do schoolwork smarter, without working harder, the students were ready to give it a try.

Since I often referred to the library as the Information Mall, I decided to use shopping for jeans as our first working problem. I wanted to see what strategies and thought processes the students would use in this familiar situation. Because I wanted all of them to work on the same problem, I made the conditions specific:

What would you do if you were shopping on your own and you need a new pair of jeans, but...

— you only want to buy Gotchas, the "in" brand of jeans;
— you have only a specific amount of money available to spend;
— you are in a new mall for the first time; and
— you have only two hours of shopping time available?

I divided the class into small groups, asked them to brainstorm the process they would take to find and buy their new jeans, and then organize those steps into only four basic activities. After five minutes of animated discussion, I asked each group to list on chart paper the steps of their procedure. I noticed, but did not discuss with the class at the time, how much prior knowledge they unconsciously used. Students often forget that they bring a solid foundation of already-known information to almost all new learning. We need to remind them that they already have links to help them process anything new.

We compared each group's process and identified the four basic steps each group had followed.
1. Determine which stores in this mall are most likely to carry Gotcha jeans.
2. Locate these stores in the mall and plan the shopping route.
3. See which store has the best bargain—the right size and style, and the best price.
4. Buy the jeans from the store that best meets your criteria (see Step 3).

When we restated those steps as a research process, they became a four-step, basic and fairly universal strategy for solving an information problem.
1. Define the specific problem.
2. Identify and locate likely resources.
3. Take notes. Organize, analyze, and summarize the information found.
4. Present the findings.

"If it's that easy," I said, "Why don't you think about how to do it for any research project? Why do I still have to walk you through the process? We need an easier way for you to know for yourself what to do, and when and how to do it."

Over the course of the next month, we discussed, relearned, examined, and evaluated many of the individual skills and strategies of the four steps. Step 4 was actually the easiest because for most problems the form of final presentation has already been specified (usually by the teacher giving the assignment). And Step 2, locating the appropriate resources (which is where most traditional library skills are concentrated), seemed to take care of itself if enough attention had been paid to Step 1. For most students the biggest stumbling block was Step 3, figuring out how to use the information they had found to create the necessary final product.

Finally, I issued a weekend challenge assignment: devise a four-letter mnemonic for our information strategy—a simple word that will help us remember the procedures to solve the problem.

At the next class session, they presented their ideas. Some were unpronounceable, while others didn't make sense. The best were workable, but didn't seem positive enough.
- Topic definition, Resources available, Information used to, Make sense = TRIM
- Narrow your target, Evaluate sources, Examine the info, Demonstrate understanding = NEED
- Subject-specific, Locate Materials, Organize Information, Put it together = SLOP
- Key words, Lots of books, Investigate, Present the results = KLIP
- Focus on topic, Locate info, Understand facts, Demonstrate understanding = FLUD
and even
- Concentrate, Research, Apply, Produce = CRAP

They were on the right track, but I was not about to endorse SLOP, FLUD or CRAP. More class discussion led to the realization that the four steps did not always have to be sequential, since the process could move both backwards and forwards as needed. More chart paper was placed on the walls, as we listed letter words for each step, trying to find a combination that made sense, made a word, and didn't offend anyone. Then someone remembered the discussion about how an experienced researcher seemed to be able to pick up a book and just *flip* it open to the right page.

- **F** OCUS on your topic.
- **L** OCATE the appropriate resources.
- **I** NVESTIGATE and I MPLEMENT the I NFORMATION you find. And finally,
- **P** RODUCE the results of your findings,

FLIP was finally christened.

I reminded the students that they still needed to include an Evaluation step in the formula, to make sure that both process and content are kept on target and answer the original question. One group thought of my use of the term I-Facts as a synonym for prior knowledge, and someone else came up with Tactical Maneuvers for thinking strategies. We all agreed that IT could also stand for Intelligent Thinking (as in, did you use your brains to best advantage?), as well as shorthand for the foundation premise of "*If* I know...*Then* I should . . . ." And so IT! was added to the "name," as both a process reminder and an evaluation checkpoint.

To validate the procedure, each student took a typical library assignment, and used FLIP IT! to explain how to solve the problem. Next, we tried FLIP-ing homework assignments from different subject classes. The students discovered that the process even worked for lab reports and math problems, by changing Locate to Logistics (specific procedure to be followed). By the end of that year, some of the students were still finding and demonstrating new ways to apply FLIP IT! to any kind of informational problem, from schoolwork to planning a swim party.

The following school year, I used FLIP IT! as the foundation for my seventh grade research skills curriculum. With a wall chart of the FLIP IT! overview on constant display, I was able to keep students on task and more focused than they had ever been before. I noticed that most of my former seventh grade students were still using the strategy whenever they had a major informational problem-solving assignment, and the eighth grade curriculum in our school included independent research projects in at least three subject areas.

That November, three of the original "FLIP-ers" came to me with a request. They had decided that if their teachers would use FLIP IT! to structure their assignments, students would be able to understand and complete those assignments more effectively. Would I design a FLIP IT! assignment worksheet for teachers to use? I suggested that the students develop it them-

selves and then help me explain how to use FLIP IT! to their teachers.
Almost all of their teachers did adopt the format for their assignments, and
have since found many ways to use it in their subject areas.

Now FLIP IT! is also used as a framework for:

Study Guide/Unit Planner:

F ocus: Unit topic, subtopics, key questions

L inks: connections to previous units studied, larger scope and
sequence

I mportant terms and concepts to be mastered

P robable test dates and kinds of evaluations

Mini-Report: (one page, bulleted format, to be displayed or
distributed to class)

Focus: brief paragraph explaining topic

Links: 1. connections to larger unit of study, other relevant topics
2. Resources used for information (bibliography)

Important Details: definitions of terms, related concepts used,
additional information

Posterity: reasons for lasting importance

Book Review:

Focus: theme or summary of plot

Layout: organization of content, literary form used

Impact: effect on reader — reaction to/involvement with characters
and events

Pass It On: other likely audiences, uses, and final reactions

Homework Assignments:

Posted on the board as follows:

Focus: unit topic, subtopic, and key questions

Lug home from locker: resources needed; e.g., textbook, study sheet,
and library books

Info involvement: assignment specifics; e.g., complete questions 1-4,
design floor plan,write essay on...

Product deadline: due date

The math teacher even translated FLIP IT! into a formula (see poster
in appendix):

F x (L+I) = P/ IT!

(FOCUS) x (LINKS & INPUT) = PAYOFF influenced by INTELLI-
GENT THINKING

to demonstrate how:

by keeping the FOCUS in mind,	F
while using both LINKS and INPUT,	L+I
the result will be an effective and intelligent PRODUCT.	P

Logistics: FLIP IT! is an Activity-based Strategy

Have you ever watched babies exploring their new world? Each new item or sensation becomes a learning experience, and most observers notice a fairly standard process during this adventure into the world of new knowledge.

1. STARE: With attention to the item and furrowed brow, the baby tries to keep the object in sight.
2. REACH FOR: "What is this? Let me at it!" Note: Stage 2 can also be RECOIL if, after a closer look, the object seems to be beyond comprehension. Think of how many small children are frightened by their first sight of a large animal or a clown. Usually the next step is:
3. TOUCH and GRAB, often followed by TASTE: "Got it! Now, what do I do with it?"
4. EXPLORATION and USE, or REJECTION: "Hmmm, this is interesting." or "Pfui!"

That instinctive process of information problem solving is the basic structure of FLIP IT! While the development of FLIP IT! is based on research-supported cognitive theory, experiential analysis, and the sequential application of higher order thinking skills strategies, it is basically an activity-centered strategy. The learner proceeds from step to step based on the fundamental question of: "IF I know this, THEN what do I need to do next?"

This use of prior knowledge is at the heart of all problem solving. I teach students to think of IF as I-FACTS—things I already know that will IMPACT (have an effect on) the situation at hand. I-Facts, therefore, are the prior knowledge about a subject that students almost always have, but all too often forget to use. By two weeks of age, a baby already has discovered the "if-then" framework:

If I make loud noises, Then someone will pay attention to me.

If I get fed, Then my stomach will feel better.

Think of all the prior knowledge about both external and internal worlds that the baby has learned, in order to know that "If I'm hungry and uncomfortable, I make noise. Then somebody takes care of me, and feeds me, so then I feel better."

FLIP IT!, therefore, is a learner-centered cognitive strategy based on the question of IF/THEN, or: What do I already know that will help me here?

Used as a mnemonic to keep the thinker on task, FLIP IT! can be applied to any form of information problem solving, whether it is a simple reference question, a more complex research project, a lab report, a math problem, or a personal quest. Each step will lead the searcher from the initial questions to the final answers by following a logical progression of critical thinking skills applied to a specific problem. The problem solver also may find it necessary to move backward or forward within the strategy as the process continues. FLIP IT! supports such a continuum of learning by providing a basic structure for the entire process. By FLIP-ing the process back to the target questions identified in the initial FOCUS step, and by keeping in mind that key operational question: IF (I know this) THEN (what can I do next)? the student can develop a plan of attack that will bring about the needed solution and final presentation.

FLIP IT!'s Four Strategic Markers:

Focus: Guideposts for the quest I'm on (specifying)   (IF...)

What is the real question or problem I'm trying to resolve?

How can I narrow my target to save time and effort?

What are the basic questions or issues I need to focus on in order to stay on task?

What facts do I need to find? (THEN...)

Links: Connections to help me proceed (strategizing)

What prior knowledge about this subject or process can I use to help me identify:

likely resources?

logical way to proceed?

layout of broader topic?

Where and how can I locate the best information?   (IF...)

How can I use these connections most efficiently?   (THEN...)

Input: Implementing the information I find (searching, sorting, sifting, and storing)

What kinds of information do I need? Why?

How do I interpret the information I acquire?

How should I record and acknowledge what I have?

How should I prioritize, categorize, organize, and utilize what I have learned?

Do I have all the information I need?   (IF...)

What additional information do I need to make sense of what I now have?

What inferences can I make? What new ideas do I now have to consider? (THEN...)

Payoff: Putting it all together for a profitable solution (sharing)

Do I have a solution to my original problem?

How can I present what I have learned?

What kind of product is required? How do I produce what was asked for?

Have I proved my ability to demonstrate my new understanding?

What kind of profit do I think I can earn from these efforts?

and finally:

IT!: Have I demonstrated Intelligent Thinking throughout the process? (IF / THEN as reflection/evaluation)

Does my final product answer my original Focus questions?

What other possibilities might I consider?

Does my final product reflect my best efforts? Why or why not?

Each step of the process uses all four of the steps within itself, either intrinsically or as an external set of checkpoints. For example: in order to take effective notes (INPUT), you must keep your FOCUS questions in mind, cite the sources you used (as part of the LINK to a broader sphere of information), decide how to categorize (IMPLEMENT) the information for most effective use, and then present the results (PAYOFF) according to the project requirements. So a student who just copies information without considering how and why to use those facts or without giving the original author credit for them, has basically FLOPped his way through this stage of the process, without a sense of direction.

Impact: Four Reasons Why FLIP IT! Has Been So Successful

Focus. FLIP IT! is learner-centered. The constant reiteration of "What do I already know, that will help me figure out what I now need to do?" reinforces the belief that the student already is a successful learner. I don't think any of the other published strategies puts enough emphasis on the use of the students' base of prior knowledge. You have to build on what is already there. What do we already know about this subject, and what do we already know about finding and using information? Telling students to use what they already know also tells them that being knowledgeable is important and valuable.

Links. FLIP IT! flows naturally from step to step, and back within itself. If you teach only parts of the process, without showing how each element is part of a unified framework, students will not see the point. It is like teaching someone how to tie shoelaces by only demonstrating how to make a loop. You must first model the process, and then walk through it several times (guided practice) before you can expect students to use it on their own (independent practice). Constant, ongoing self-evaluation of both process and product is an integral part of the strategy. At each step, the learner needs to focus on the original concerns, to make sure the target questions are being answered and acted upon. Each step, therefore, links naturally and reasonably both into the next step and back to the beginning.

Implementation. FLIP IT! serves as a guide to help students develop the skills they need to become
  • Goal-oriented (WHAT do I need to accomplish?)
  • Purposeful and productive (WHY do I need to do this?)
  • Strategic and self-evaluative (HOW will I know what to do? HOW well did I succeed?)
effective learners, thinkers, and problem solvers.

Although FLIP IT! can be applied to all kinds of situations, I never introduce it to students as a unique process or set of skills. Instead, I use FLIP IT! to solve a genuine information need, demonstrating its use as an efficient framework for working through an already-assigned problem. As we're working through the problem, I repeatedly ask "OK, IF we know this, THEN what do we need to do/figure out next?" Only after we have used the process several times do I point out that this is a generic strategy that can be

Got a problem to solve?

FLIP IT!

Focus:
Stop and think! Identify specifics.

Link:
What do you already know?

Input:
Implement the Information you find.

Payoff:
Put it all together

for

Intelligent Thinking!

Reproducible from *FLIP IT! An Information Skills Strategy for Student Researchers* by Alice H. Yucht (1997, Linworth Publishing, Inc.)

Figure 1.1

FLIP IT! An Information Skills Strategy for Student Researchers

used for all kinds of problems. I display posters that say: "FLIP IT! for successful problem solving," and I will often remind students who have already used the process to FLIP IT! when they are "stuck" at some stage of any other info-problem. Because we have been using FLIP IT! to help us find answers in all subject areas, it becomes an easily transferable process for students to use in many ways.

Product. FLIP IT! uses everyday language. The process does involve task definition, search strategies, information assessment, and even synthesis and evaluation, but I have never heard students use such terminology on their own. The original mnemonic created by that first group of seventh graders was "Focus, Locations, Information Implementation, and Product". Over the years of development and use, the original words have sometimes changed to meet specific situations, but the letters are the same, reflecting the four basic steps of the problem-solving process.

Payoff: Uses and Spin-offs

Since its beginnings, FLIP IT! has taken on a life of its own as I demonstrate its generic possibilities to teachers and librarians in my workshops. We've discovered all kinds of instructional tie-ins as FLIP IT! has been used to:

- expand current learning activities and strategies in all subject areas.
- restructure courses of study for more in-depth and interdisciplinary coverage.
- develop effective strategies to maximize student learning.
- infuse critical thinking and problem-solving skills into all lessons.
- develop, supervise, and evaluate cooperative projects and activities.
- design rubrics for authentic assessment of student learning.
- reinforce practical learning strategies for special needs students.
- design effective lessons for information skills mastery.
- develop resource-based learning activities across the curriculum.
- organize collaborative efforts across all subject strands.

For example:

- Librarians and classroom teachers use it as a collaborative template for developing resource-based learning activities.
- A reviews editor considers it an effective way to structure a book evaluation—and to explain to new reviewers what to consider.
- An eighth grade social studies teacher teaches his classes to use FLIP IT! to construct their responses to essay questions. A high school teacher uses it as a simple acronym for teaching her students the scientific process in biology.
- A debate coach insists that his students FLIP all their research and preparation, so they won't "flap at the mouth and flop in the scoring" during the actual debates.
- A preservice supervisor uses it as a framework to teach student teachers how to think through and structure a lesson plan.
- A curriculum coordinator uses it to reorganize major units within a subject area.

Four years after I started teaching students to FLIP IT!, I got a call from Father Joe, the Chairman of the English Department at a prestigious Catholic high school attended by many of my former students. The faculty there had noted that my former students were well-prepared for high school work. They were comfortable doing independent research, able to think through information problems, and better at constructing essays. Over the years, it has been traditional at this high school for students to write the letters J M J in the upper right corner of tests and term papers as an abbreviation for the prayer, "Jesus, Mary, and Joseph, help me in my hour of need." Father Joe told me that for the past two years he had noticed that my former students were writing F L I P in the upper left corner of their essay papers. When questioned, they explained that they had been taught to use it as a checklist for organizing their thoughts. But then one day he received a paper with F L I P in the corner from a student who had not gone to my school. The student finally admitted that he had no idea what the letters stood for, but "Ryan writes them on all his papers, and he always gets good grades, so they must work somehow!"

I can't guarantee that FLIP IT! will work as a successful incantation for your students. But by showing them how to use FLIP IT! as a generic strategy for any kind of complex informational activity, we can teach students a process for successful problem solving in any kind of situation.

Library Skills and Information Literacy

Ken Haycock often tells school librarians ". . . do not talk about *Library Skills* — for most [outsiders], dusting and shelving is what comes to mind." (from a speech at the Educational Media Association of New Jersey annual conference, December 8, 1994)

What librarians teach is most appropriately called information literacy. We do it by teaching students how to become confident consumers of the wealth of ideas available not just in the library, but throughout the constantly expanding world of information in our technological universe.

Cathy-Mae Karelse and Peter G. Underwood, in their articles about the information superhighway in *Higher Education Review* describe information literacy as ". . . a set of transferable skills which allow users to identify their information problems and needs, access required information irrespective of source or channel, use and evaluate the information...[Today's] move away from teacher centred to learner centred approaches sharpens the need to inculcate skills of assessment and evaluation of information, and emphasizes the importance of knowing how to link new information to existing models. Imagine driving along the highway. In the rear seat is someone giving you directions. As you drive you are experiencing one route to a destination. Now imagine being given a map and instructions on how it can be used. It becomes possible to see many routes to the same destination and many other destinations. We must enable people to develop beyond managing to drive, to become competent navigators." (Karelse, 1996)

Many of our state organizations have already developed information literacy curriculums articulating the same basic concepts and skills, e.g.,

"Students will develop the ability to

1. Articulate Information Needs: know when to question, what to question, and how to question.
2. Identify Appropriate Information: locate, access, evaluate, and select textual, numeric, and visual information as needed.
3. Use Information: manipulate, analyze, organize, and interpret information and apply this information to concepts already known.
4. Communicate Information: present the results of analysis in the best format for the type of communication and audience.
5. Assess the Learning: evaluate the effectiveness of both the process and the product."

(Minnesota Educational Media Organization, 1992)

FLIP IT! is not a curriculum; I have used it only as a conceptual framework to redefine and reorganize the traditional individual units of a broader foundation of generic information problem-solving skills. Standard scope-and-sequence curricula stratify the skills to be taught into discrete units, organized by content and format into both grade and mastery levels, e.g. using encyclopedias for research will be introduced in second grade, reinforced in fourth grade, and expanded in sixth grade. FLIP IT! is used as a process-oriented framework, presenting skills as they become relevant and applicable based on the learner's need to understand and use the content and format. Each unit is developed both within the context of use, as appropriate to the cognitive abilities of the learners, and also as part of a continuum of problem-solving strategies and applications. Many of the individual units may belong in more than one category, depending upon the particular context and application of the strategy.

FLIP IT! is simply a strategy for effective thinking, helping students understand that to THINK means to:

Tie
History (old knowledge, information)
Into
New
Knowledge

and that THINKING also requires the

T H U(nderstanding) N K
T H E(valuating) and R(etaining) N K, and
T H A(pplying) N K
of whatever you have just learned.

Key Elements of the Learning Process: Meaning, Motivation, and Metacognition

One April my school library was inundated with students busily reading and taking notes from the medical encyclopedias, all suffering from the dreaded "disease" assignment in Health class in which each student had to research and then present an oral report on a different contagious disease. What amazed me was that in spite of all the information these students were so industriously copying, most of them could not tell me how they would know if they actually had the disease. In other words, although they had just written the symptoms, they still could not isolate and identify them out of context.

Critical thinking skills are often considered a universal panacea in curriculum development circles. But everyone has a different definition of the term, and a different schema or set of skills in mind. Whether they're called cognitive skills, higher order thinking skills, problem-solving skills, formal logic processes, metacognitive approaches, or information literacy, these "new" skills frameworks deal with the access, identification, use, evaluation, and production of information; an emphasis on process (the skills used) over product (the knowledge acquired).

Yet today's students are expected to demonstrate knowledge of the WHAT (the product, or answers to a question) without also demonstrating any fundamental understanding of the HOW and WHY (the process, or strategies and procedures used to arrive at that answer). As the information specialists, it is our job to help today's learners become tomorrow's thinkers. By teaching students to be conscious of the processes involved in learning, we help them develop the ability to think carefully, critically, and creatively about the world around them.

Most successful learning/thinking frameworks are based on basic cognitive assumptions (Jones, 1987), but I group these basic assumptions into the "3 M's."

Meaning
Meaning is the learners' prior knowledge, using what they already know in order to make sense of the new information.

Learning involves conneccting new information to prior knowledge. Students process new information most effectively when it can be related to something they already know.
EXAMPLE:
Focus: Fiction books are arranged alphabetically by the author's last name.
Links: Students already understand:
    alphabetical order
    that their own names are listed alphabetically by last name in a
    phone book or on the attendance sheet.
Payoff: Students will be able to locate fiction books by a specific author.

Learning is influenced by development. Students' individual stages of chronological, intellectual and emotional development affect the skills and learning they can demonstrate.
EXAMPLE:
Focus: Boolean operators can help target an online database search.
Links: Students already understand:
    Databases as compilations of information
    Use of key words as search terms
Input: Students will learn how to use AND, OR, and NOT as Boolean
    operators.

Payoff: Students will construct an effective and efficient search strategy.

Motivation
Motivation is the learner's need to master this new information or, why nobody ever chooses to fail Driver's Ed.

Learning is goal-oriented. Students will explore sources of information more readily when they have a reason for using that information.
EXAMPLE:
Focus: The OPAC can be used to locate books on a specific topic.
Link: Students already understand how to use key words as search terms.
Payoff: Student finds useful information about caring for his new gerbil.

Learning is influenced by both intrinsic and extrinsic rewards. Students will be more likely to learn, when they understand the benefits of that learning.
EXAMPLE:
Focus: Use of color affects emotional reaction to a visual image.
Link: Students need to design posters for a contest.
Payoff: The student with the most eye-catching poster wins a $50 prize.

Metacognition
Metacognition is the learners' active use of thinking strategies, knowing how to organize and restructure the new information in order to use it effectively.

Learning involves organizing information. Most knowledge can be arranged or categorized into some kind of recognizable pattern. These patterns may be either generic (common to all subjects) or specific (purely content-related).
EXAMPLE:
Focus: Students will create a timeline of Revolutionary War battles.
Links: Students already understand:
       use of time-order as an organizing strategy
       basic history of the Revolutionary War
Input: Students will gather information about specific battles and dates.
Payoff: Students will record information about each battle at appropriate points along a model representing the duration of the Revolutionary War.

Learning is strategy-dependent. Students will need to use previously-mastered skills and procedures in order to develop their understanding of the new knowledge.
EXAMPLE:
Focus: Farenheit and Celsius are two different ways of measuring temperature.
Links: Students already understand that:
       temperature can be measured.
       different scales can be used for measuring similar properties.
Input: Students will learn how each scale is used.

Payoff: Students will:

compare and contrast the reasons for using each scale.

develop a conversion scale for measuring in either Farenheit or Celsius.

Learning is both linear (sequential) and nonlinear. Most learning occurs in three phases:

1. anticipation (defining the need or identifying the focus),
2. activation (integrating new information with prior knowledge), and
3. application (using what has just been processed).

Extending the new learning can happen at any stage of learning, and may even go off on a different tangent than originally considered.

EXAMPLE:

Focus: Desert regions have unique characteristics.

Link: Students are studying geomes, the regions of the earth.

Input: Students will:

brainstorm what they already know about deserts.

research information about specific deserts around the world.

identify commonalities of landforms and weather conditions for all deserts.

Payoff: Students will prepare a report on the major characteristics of desert regions.

Links: Students will investigate other regions, and eventually prepare reports comparing and contrasting the characteristics of all terrestrial geomes.

Students will compare the characteristics of other planets to earth, identifying more universal geomes.

Students will design the "ideal" geome for human existence in the 21st century.

It is up to us as librarians and teachers to teach students how to access, use, evaluate, and produce information, as well as how to appreciate all kinds of cultural formats, in order to be prepared for the InfoTech world of their future. So when learned "authorities" decide to review your curriculum, and examine its relevance to some newly-devised core content curriculum standards, don't flinch. After all, we have been using these techniques all along, even before they were prescribed!

FLIP IT! for Effective Lesson Planning

"The only true measure of education is to look at how kids have taken what they've learned in school and applied it to real-life situations." — Rae Ellen McKee, 1990 National Teacher of the Year.

Teaching any subject would be easy if all we had to do was deliver the information, demonstrate the skill, and have the students take it from there. But in the real world of education, nothing is ever that easy. Instead, we have to decide how complex this information or skill will be for students to master; develop an effective and efficient way to present the material, and then determine whether students are understanding and mastering the learning unit as we are presenting it. Regardless of the topic, students will learn more when teachers' plans reflect the following concerns:

LEARNING OBJECTIVES = The specific information (content) and/or skill (process) students will learn and demonstrate at this time

Learning = content (information) + process (skill)

Objective = learning + behavior

Behavior = demonstration of understanding

A handy mnemonic to keep in mind while developing learning objectives is:

A = Audience (the learner's characteristics; e.g., sixth grade students)

B = Behavior (what the learner will demonstrate; e.g., will use the Reader's Guide to find magazine articles on a topic)

C = Conditions (situations and requirements that affect the behavior and the learning opportunity; e.g., in one class period, working individually)

D = Degree of success (what will be considered an acceptable demonstration of mastery/understanding; e.g., student will find at least three useful articles on their topic)

Preparation

Planning and preparing effective lessons takes both effort and time. Even those unplanned lessons that turn out to be instant successes are really the result of prior thought about each of the following:

Focus. On what specific skill, information, concept, or idea do I want this activity to concentrate? In order to identify the focus, you first must know:

• why your students need to learn this, and

• what prior knowledge or skill they must have mastered in order to understand this unit.

Logistics. What arbitrary factors will affect how I design the activity I want to use? These factors can include:

• Facility and materials: special forms, equipment, set-ups, or prior arrangements, such as:

1. worksheets
2. audio-visual hardware and software
3. special collection of books or props
4. special room or furniture arrangement

• Number of students involved.

• Time frames: Even the most effective teaching strategies won't be successful if you don't have adequate time to teach and students don't have adequate time to learn. For every lesson, take into account the following time constraints:

• Available time: How long and how often will the class have to be in the library to learn this information? How much contact time can be allocated for this activity?

• Structured time: Provide adequate learning time for each lesson by establishing and maintaining efficient classroom/library routines that save time and eliminate disruptions and distractions.

• Instructional/Engaged time: Also known as time on task, this means the amount of time that students are actively engaged in learning the lesson objective, whether through direct instruction, guided practice, or independent practice. Remember that instruction does not automatically translate to learning. Students must DO to LEARN. How much time will you have to both present the material and monitor student learning? Calculate the length of the scheduled class period, minus time spent on transitions, book exchange, and locating resources. Remember that students often learn better and more easily by working with and helping each other.

Implementation. What should happen and in what order? Keep in mind the:
- Specific activities to be utilized. Introduce lessons with a relevant "teaser" from the library collection to pique students' curiosity and motivation to learn.
- Prior learning to be reviewed. Always relate new material to students' prior knowledge or personal experiences. This gives them a better frame of reference and facilitates transfer of learning.
- Modeling of behavior and directions to be given. Demonstrate the skills and strategies needed. Show students how you would work through the problem.
- Students' learning abilities. The slower the learner, the smaller each subskill or task should be. Ask questions that require processing or application of the new knowledge, not just simple recall.
- Variety of teaching and learning styles.
    1. Proceed in small steps at a brisk pace to maximize student involvement and minimize distractions and disruptions.
    2. Use a variety of techniques to engage student response.
    3. Focus on one thought/subskill/point at a time, avoid digressions, and organize the lesson so that each subskill is mastered before you move on.
    4. Give specific instructions and detailed explanations. Check for understanding at each step. Always make sure that students are with you before moving forward.
    5. Interact constantly with students through direct eye contact and questioning.

Proof. How do you measure whether the objective was achieved? Also identify:
- remediation procedures, if necessary.
- any follow-up activities.
- ways to improve the procedure.
- other concerns relevant to this unit.

Keep that reminder for **IT!**: Intelligent Thinking as an evaluation marker throughout the process. Also keep in mind that all learning activities should be "S.M.A.R.T.":

Specific: focuses on no more than three well-defined and manageable objectives,

Measurable: includes specific goals (how much, how many, how well) for each required activity,

Attainable: takes into account the learner's real abilities,

Results Centered: has a demonstrable "product",

Time Bound: has specific parameters for learning, application, and use.

FLIP IT! can be used as a basic framework for developing lesson plans and collaborative activities since no matter what skill is being taught, effective instructional design requires the teacher and/or librarian to:

- identify the FOCUS of each lesson,
- utilize the LINKS to content, students' prior knowledge, and applicability,
- structure the INPUT and IMPLEMENTATION required to make sure that students learn how to use the skill, and
- assess the PROOF or demonstration of the students' understanding and application of the particular skill.

Lesson/Activity Planning Outline

Focus:

    A. Target Objectives: What skills or content will this lesson cover?

    B. Rationale: Why is this skill or content needed at this time?

Links/Logistics: What will I need to know or do in advance to make this lesson work?

    A. Prior knowledge/skills the learner should already have mastered

    B. Materials needed

    C. Teaching area/facility setup

    D. Time constraints

Input/Implementation: How will I structure this lesson to maximize student understanding?

    A. Introduction — reason for skill use; hook or motivator

    B. Modeling — demonstration by teacher

        1. level of complexity

        2. sequencing of steps

    C. Guided Practice — scaffolding by teacher; small group work

        1. segmentation of practice

        2. variety of examples

        3. feedback/reactions

        4. built-in success

    D. Independent Practice — individual application

        1. authentic problems

        2. variety of examples

        3. levels of difficulty

    E. Closure: wrap-up and review, as well as teaser for next activity.

Payoff/Proof: How will I assess individual student mastery of this skill?
- A. Grading rubrics
- B. Remediation indicators
- C. Demonstration format
  and IT!: Evaluation of INTELLIGENT THINKING: How will I know that students have retained this skill?
- A. Continued demonstration of skill mastery
- B. Additional skills which reinforce this process or content
- C. Applications in other areas.

Sample Activity Plan

Students are learning how different kinds of materials are organized and arranged in the library. Today's activity is about biography call numbers and arrangement. This is a LINKS activity since students will be learning how to locate biographies. (Note: This is a generic activity about call numbers that can be used for other book genres.)

Focus: Biography Call Numbers and Shelf Arrangement.
- A. Target Objectives: What skills or content will this lesson cover?
  1. Skills: location of biographies based on either call number or subject name
  2. Content: construction of a biography call number
- B. Rationale: Why is this skill or content needed at this time?
  1. Students will be reading biographies in Language Arts unit on informational writing.
  2. Students need to know how to locate and use library materials.

Links/Logistics. What will I need to know or do in advance to make this lesson work?
- A. Prior knowledge/skills the learner should already have mastered:
  1. Alphabetical arrangement by person's last name
  2. Biography format as chronological information about a person's life
- B. Materials needed:
  1. Several new biographies to use as teasers
  2. Bookcover worksheets with marked spaces for author, title, and call number (Note: This is a generic worksheet that can be used for any kind of call number activity.)
  3. Chalkboard, overhead projector, or chart paper for teacher/ librarian use
- C. Teaching area/facility set up:
  1. Six work tables with four students per table
  2. "Magic" bookshelf marked out on floor with masking tape
- D. Time constraints:
  One 40-minute period

Input/Implementation. How will I structure this lesson to maximize student understanding?

A. Introduction:

1. Briefly booktalk two or three new biographies, while keeping call numbers covered. Explain that the library just got these books, and they haven't been shelved yet. Where do students think these books should be shelved and why?
2. Discuss characteristics of biographies. Which is more important: author or subject? Why?

Part 1: Constructing a Biography Call Number:

(Modeling)

1. Explain that libraries give biographies a special kind of call number (B on top, first three letters of last name on bottom) in order to put books about the same person together. Use sample worksheet (on chalkboard, overhead transparency or chart paper) to demonstrate, using information for one of the teaser books. Show actual spine label on book.
2. Repeat, asking class to create call number for another teaser book.

(Guided practice)

3. Have class construct sample biography call numbers for books about classmates or teachers. Write these samples in random order on blank chalkboard.
4. Ask class to silently think of a famous person each would like to "biographize—interview, follow around, and then write that person's life story."
5. Distribute bookcover worksheets. Have students write their own names in the space for "author," and the name of their famous person in the space for "title."

(Independent Practice)

6. Briefly review how to construct a biography call number. Have students construct and write the call number for their "book" on their worksheet. Circulate among students, checking for accuracy. Tell students to turn papers face down after they have been checked.

Part 2: Arranging/locating biographies by call number:

(Introduction)

1. Briefly review the function of call numbers as location devices or addresses. Ask students how they think biographies might be arranged.
2. Have students look at sample call numbers on board. Obviously, they're not in correct order.

(Guided practice)

3. Ask class to help put call numbers in correct order. Write the correct sequence on the board.

4. Have students turn worksheets face up, and hold them up at chest height like open books, with "cover" information facing out.
5. Explain that you want students to "shelve" themselves in correct order on the "magic bookshelf" line you've marked on the floor. Remind students that books cannot talk, so this must be done silently, by looking at each other's call numbers, and deciding where they fit. (Note: There will almost always be some duplicates. This gives you the opportunity to demonstrate and reinforce arrangement first by subject, then by author.)
6. Check "shelf" for accuracy, asking students to help with any corrections.

(Individual practice)
1. Have students insert their worksheets into the appropriate locations on the actual biography shelves.
2. Supervise and assist as necessary. Students may look for books to borrow after they have shelved their worksheets correctly.

Payoff/Proof and Evaluation of Intelligent Thinking.
A. How will I be able to assess individual student mastery of this skill?
1. Process: informal observation and assessment of student ability to follow directions and complete the activity independently
2. Content: accurate information on the worksheet
B. How will I know that students have retained this skill?
1. Continued demonstration of skill mastery
• Students will be able to locate and shelve other biographies, given either the call number or the name of the subject of the book.
• Students will be able to line up for dismissal in correct shelf order for the biographies they have just checked out to read.
2. Additional skills that build on/reinforce this process/content
• Students will understand that a person's last name can be used as a key word to locate information.

Chapter 2

Links: FLIP IT! As Library/Information Skills Framework

R. J. Marzano's *Dimensions of Thinking*, and later . . . *Dimensions of Learning* describe an instructional model that "is structured on the premise that the process of learning involves the interaction of five types, or dimensions, of thinking:
1. Positive attitudes and perceptions about learning,
2. Thinking involved in acquiring and integrating knowledge,
3. Thinking involved in extending and refining knowledge,
4. Thinking involved in using knowledge meaningfully, and
5. Productive habits of mind." (Marzano, 1992)

As Library/Information Specialists, we can see how these dimensions are reflected in our own curricula.
1. Positive attitudes and perceptions about the library as a comfortable, welcoming place to use for all kinds of learning, both informational and recreational
2. Location and access skills, as well as information usage (note taking, organizing, and summarizing) skills
3. Application, integration, and analysis skills, such as comparing data, evaluating relevancy, and analyzing relationships
4. Synthesis and production skills, such as presenting the results of the investigation and completing a project
5. Evaluation skills, in order to recognize the quality of a project, demonstrate retention of a skill, assess the efficiency of the process, or determine further usefulness or other applications

FLIP IT! can be used as a framework for reorganizing the traditional library skills curriculum to reflect the more holistic scope of information literacy skills.

Focus Skills — Zooming in on the Subject
Defining the problem
Narrowing the subject of investigation
Specific subtopics/key search terms to consider
Informational formats and genres

Sample Skills Units:
>Key Words
>Narrowing a Topic
>Types of Questions/Response Formats
>Publication Formats

Links/Location Skills — Finding the Detailed Information Needed

Types of Resources
>Print
>Electronic
>Personal

Access points to resources
Evaluating and selecting appropriate resources
Connections to additional possibilities
Sample Skills Units:
>Resource Formats
>Print vs. Electronic Resources
>Search Strategies
>Indexes and Search Engines
>Concept Analysis

Input/Information Usage Skills

Interpreting/Implementing the Information — using what you find
>Acquiring information:
>>Evaluating the facts
>>Taking notes
>>Citing sources
>Evaluating information
>Integrating information from a variety of sources
>Organizing and categorizing the information acquired
>Sample Skills Units:
>>Note Taking
>>Outlining/Diagramming/Graphic Organizers
>>Bibliographic Citations
>>Fact vs. Opinion
>>Primary vs. Secondary Sources
>>Literature Appreciation Activities

Payoff/Presentation Skills: Putting It All Together

>Kind of product needed
>"Repackaging" of information
>Organization of presentation
>Evaluation of results
>Sample Skills Units:
>>Preparing Bibliographies
>>Presentation Formats

In many cases the skills overlap, and a specific activity will use all four elements of FLIP IT! in its development. That's what makes FLIP IT! so useful: it is contantly being used to structure both the process and the content of each learning unit.

Application and Examples
In order to give a framework to the samples for each of the FLIP IT! elements, I have used specific information skills activities from an interdisciplinary grade-level project. This middle-school curriculum is about world patterns of geography. Areas of study include:
- physical geography, including location, climate, topography, resources, human-environmental interactions, regional conditions, and map and globe skills
- personal geography, including history, political and social institutions, economics, literature, lifestyles, and communication skills

While the primary focus is on Social Studies and Language Arts, connections to the Science, Math, Literature, Arts and Technology curriculums are also made wherever possible.

For this project, each student will investigate a different country and present the information found to the class. All of the project activities have been been planned jointly by the classroom teachers and the librarian. The Social Studies teacher will oversee subject content; the Language Arts teacher will supervise and evaluate any writing processes; the Computer Tech teacher will teach necessary production skills for all reports; and the Librarian will provide most of the informational resources to be used, teach any necessary research skills, and coordinate all project timelines. Resources used will include standard print materials, multi-media and online resources, materials from outside sources such as embassies and travel agents, and personal interviews. Students will use individual project folders for all worksheets, activity guides, and checklists necessary for completion of the project.

To stretch students' creative abilities and to prevent "cut and paste" reports, the standard research project format has been changed to reflect students' fascination with interplanetary adventure.

FOCUS: Scouting Reports to the Territorial Commissioner: Students are the advance team investigating an "alien" (foreign) civilization, for possible settlement and assimilation.
LINKS: Based on their study and knowledge of the elements of their own (American) civilization, students will investigate and report on commonalities and differences in the "alien" civilization and culture.
INPUT: Information on five major aspects of this "alien" territory: physical geography, personal lifestyles, economics, politics and government, and recreational activities
PRODUCTS:
- Letters sent "home" to the Territorial Commissioner every other week, reporting on various aspects of the new civilization

- Investigative documentation, including:
  bibliographies of resources used
  field notes (worksheets, charts, and additional assignments)
- Exhibit booth at the annual Territorial "Expedition Expo," demonstrating artifacts and souvenirs acquired during the scouting expedition, and presenting arguments for settlement in this new location.

The entire project has been broken down into smaller, topical units to keep students on task.

- First impressions: physical location and landmarks (as noted by traveler from "afar")
- Blending in: personal life, including language, customs, religion, and lifestyle
- Income and Expenses: economics, including monetary system, resources and manufacturing, employment
- Who's in charge: politics and government, educational system, and current issues
- Having fun: recreational activities, including sports, entertainment

After explanations of the general guidelines, terminology, activities, recommended resources, and product formats to be used, timelines are set up for each of the above units, with target dates for:

- specific activities, assignments, and skills lessons,
- research time (both in school and out),
- computer lab time for production of all final reports, and
- submission of each topical report and relevant field notes

as well as the final project display at the Expedition Expo.

Focus Activities

Focus means defining the problem at hand, by determining:

- What is the specific quest I am on or problem I am trying to resolve?
- How can I best narrow my target to save time and effort?
- What are the basic questions and issues I need to focus on in order to stay on task?
- What kinds of facts do I really need to find?
- What do I already know, that will help me?

Think of focus as the "zoom-in" stage, when you use a magnifier to identify the elements of the subject that require closer examination. Focusing provides the trail markers to navigate through the maze of information. Understanding how to define the problem is the most important skill for successful problem-solving.

Students often have difficulty finding information because they don't know what they are looking for. They haven't done any preparatory thinking about the problem, pausing to identify the kinds of information needed and the most efficient way to find it. Without a clearly-defined focus, the information search becomes confusing and frustrating to the student.

(Unfortunately, many teachers fail to recognize the importance of this step when assigning problems. They assume that everyone in the class understands the focus of the assignment, when the opposite often is true.)

Defining the problem keeps the target issue at the center of all activities by serving as a checkpoint for the strategies involved in the other stages of the problem solving process. The links must be relevant for the target questions; the input acquired must answer the target questions; and the payoff must provide a resolution to the original focus. Focus skills units include:

Materials Formats:
- Fiction
- NonFiction
- Biography
- Illustrated/picture books
- Visuals: posters, charts, graphs, and maps
- Reference section
- Periodicals and vertical file materials
- AV software and hardware
- Electronic formats and hardware

Information Approaches:
- Task Definition
- Selecting and formulating a topic
- Narrowing a subject
- Key words
- Informational frameworks:
  1. Categories of information
  2. Arrangements of information
  3. Patterns of information use
  4. Publication and presentation conventions

Informational Frameworks

As librarians, we work with information in many different forms so the possibilities for re-organizing data into different categories, patterns, and genres seem self-evident to us. When we teach students that information can restructured into different frames of reference based on how that information will be used, we are forcing them to look at facts as connections of ideas, not as isolated bits of data.

Information Categories. How many times have students been told to identify the "Ws"—who, what, when, where, and why—to write a report about an event? Some reading and language experts refer to this as giving information a story setting. For students to see the value and function of these bits of information as part of a larger framework, we need to explain the interconnections of those categories and how they define all areas of human experience.

Who was involved? What events took place? When and where did it happen? Why? The linking of time, environment, participants, action, and motive makes the information about this experience coherent. Unless data is placed into one of these categories, it is basically meaningless. For example, if the answer is "lunch", what was the question?—What did Sue bring? When are you going to see him? Why were you in that room? Grouping facts into these separate yet interrelated categories gives students an easily understood and universally adaptable framework to use for gathering and then restructuring information.

Information Arrangements. Most information questions require answers that arrange the data into some kind of connecting pattern. Teach students how to recognize and apply the four basic types of information arrangements that organize data into a pattern or format based on the connections that link the individual bits of data, and they will be able to formulate both questions and answers more effectively.

The four types of information arrangements are lists, time-order, cause-effect, and compare-contrast.

- Lists are groups of facts, ideas, people, places, or things whose only connection is that they have something in common.
    - NAME several kinds of cars.
    - LIST all the kids in your class.
    - IDENTIFY five different kinds of music.
    - WHICH teams are in the National League?
- Time-order questions require an understanding of the sequence of events — the order in which something happened.
    - Who was the THIRD President?
    - WHEN do we have lunch?
    - What is your daily SCHEDULE?
    - HOW DO you build a tree house?
- Cause-effect answers explain how or why something happens.
    - HOW did the building catch fire?
    - WHY do leaves turn colors?
    - Give four REASONS FOR the Revolutionary War.
    - WHAT WILL HAPPEN if you don't pass this test?
- Compare-contrast questions ask for the similarities or differences that qualify several equivalent or corresponding items.
    - Explain the THREE branches of government.
    - Who is your BEST friend?
    - What is the DIFFERENCE between the Republican and Democrat parties?
    - Why did you CHOOSE this brand of soda?

For example, given the request to "Describe this country's most important holidays," the reporter must consider:
Focus: Which format should I use?
- List: Give the name and brief description of each event.
- Time-order: Tell when they take place, and when they were first observed
- Cause-effect: Explain how and why they are celebrated.
- Compare-contrast: Is this a local version of Independence Day or New Year's Day?

Links: Are these holidays cultural, geographic, historical, religious, or political?

Input: What kinds of facts and how much detail do I need to give about each of the specific holidays?

Product: How should I present this information—in a calendar, show-n-tell, or as part of another subtopic?

Understanding these information frameworks will help students devise more effective FOCUS questions to guide them in their own investigations.

Sample Focus Activity:
Identifying Search Terms

This activity can be done by the teacher in the classroom before coming to the library or by the librarian as a warm-up or review in the library before the research starts. By narrowing the subject of investigation and identifying key search terms to use in advance, students will be more successful and efficient in their research, and less likely to get sidetracked by other details.

This lesson focuses only on developing a pre-search strategy to make it easier to access the needed information. Other aspects of the research activity—choosing appropriate resources, taking notes, and selecting a presentation format—are not the focus of this lesson. Those link, input and pay-off skills may have been developed at another time or will be addressed as the unit progresses and the need arises.

Activity Plan
Focus: Identify key words to use for research about the politics of a country.
Links/Logistics:

    A. Prior knowledge/skills:

        1. using key words to locate information efficiently

        2. basic concepts and terminology about politics and government

    B. Materials needed:

        1. Standard classroom with blackboard, chart paper or overhead projector

        2. Focus Frames worksheet

        3. Posterboard or chart paper

    C. Facility set-up: standard classroom arrangement

    D. Time constraints: 15-20 minutes

Input/Implementation:

    1. Using Focus Frames worksheet, have class brainstorm and review basic terminology regarding politics and government. (executive, judicial, legislative, laws, monarchy, senate, assembly, courts, military)

    2. Record all terms suggested on blackboard.

    3. Discuss and regroup terms into sub-topics of related categories of information. Have the class record information on the worksheet as the teacher writes it on the board.

    4. Explain the use of these terms as key words or subject descriptors when looking for information. Discuss and identify the most likely key words and synonyms (subtopic terms) to be found in resources.

Product/Proof:

    1. Make and display an instant reference poster of KEY WORDS to be used during research.

FOCUS FRAMES:
ZOOMING IN ON THE SUBJECT

DIRECTIONS:

1. Brainstorm and write down possible subtopics and questions about your topic in the big frame.

2. Identify the related topics within the big frame.

3. Re-organize (group and rewrite) these subtopics into the small frames.

4. Write useful key words/search terms for each subtopic on the lines next to the small frames.

SUB-TOPIC:

SUB-TOPIC:

SUB-TOPIC:

SUB-TOPIC:

Figure 2.1 Focus Frames Worksheet

2. The poster will be displayed while the class is doing research. Remind students to use their own Focus Frames worksheets as working guides and to add to their worksheets new terms they encounter.

Closure — Intelligent Thinking:

Brainstorm posssible resources to be used, and review how to use the Key Words to access information in those resources.

Students will use Focus Frames worksheets to develop search terms for each unit of investigation. Sometimes the activity will be done as a group, and sometimes it will be completed independently. All of their worksheets will become part of their field notes, kept in their project folders, and graded as part of the total project.

Links Activities

Links are the connections used to find the information needed to solve the problem. Links use the two foundation questions that underscore all the strategies:

• What do I already know that will help me? and

• What are my target questions—the focus I need to keep in mind?

in order to answer the questions:

• Where and how can I look for the best information to use?

• How can I use these connections most efficiently?

This is the stage most commonly recognized as traditional location and access skills. But links are more than just an examination of different resources. Links include the logistics of problem solving, from resource selection and evaluation to the development of both simple and complex search strategies.

Links units include:

• Library facilities and layouts

• Types of Resources :

• Print Formats

  • Books

    • Fiction

    • Nonfiction

    • Picture books

  • Reference section, including:

    • Encyclopedias

    • Dictionaries and thesauri

    • Almanacs and handbooks

    • Atlases

    • Periodicals, pamphlets, and newsletters

• Multi-media formats, including:

  • Visuals, such as posters, maps, paintings, and charts

  • AV software

  • Microforms

• Electronic Formats

  • Computer software

  • CD-ROMs

  • Online databases including OPACs

  • Internet and World Wide Web

• Personal

  • Interviews

  • TV/radio

  • Speeches, presentations

  • Letters, memos, and e-mail

• Access points to resources

  • Print formats:

    • Cataloging systems such as DDC and LC

    • Card catalogs

    • Parts of the book, such as indexes and tables of contents

    • Periodical indexes

- Electronic formats:
  - OPACs
  - Search engines
  - Dialog
- Search Strategies:
  - Skimming and scanning
  - Boolean searching
  - Concept Analysis
  - Expanding and refining topics
- Evaluating and selecting appropriate resources
  - Accuracy and authority
  - Primary vs. secondary sources
  - Information coverage and currency
  - Citing information resources

The primary function of all LINKS units is to get the student to the most useful and appropriate information to solve the FOCUS problem. LINKS are "seeking and selection" activities. What the seeker does with the acquisition and implementation of the information is the next stage in the total problem-solving process—INPUT.

Evaluating Resources

Teaching students how to select the best resource for a particular use has always been part of a Library/Information Skills curriculum. Technology has added a new dimension to this area with the proliferation of new formats for resources, such as CD-ROMs, laser discs, online databases, and Web sites. Now that almost anyone with access to a computer, a modem, and some simple software can mount a Web page, we have to teach students how to evaluate these new forms of information distribution, instead of assuming that because it has been "produced" it is acceptable or verifiable or even accurate.

Evaluating a Web Page. Just as a Web page is a non-linear presentation, so too is the process of evaluation. Specific criteria have been grouped into the four strands of FLIP only as an organizational schema. During the evaluation process, many of the considerations will overlap.

Focus: Why? Who?
- Purpose:

  Why is this information online?

  Who is the intended audience?
- Authority/Validity:

  Who wrote or produced this site?

  Is contact information for the author or producer provided?

  What proof of authority or expertise is given?

  How reliable is the information presented?

  How current is the information? How often is it revised?

Links: How?
- Ease of Navigation:
  - How is the site organized?
  - Are there loops from the home page to supporting pages and back?
  - Are links logically grouped?
- Use of links:
  - Is there consistency and clarity of icons?
  - Are there any blind links or moved sites?
  - Are the links relevant and appropriate?
  - Is there a balance between inlinks (within this site) and outlinks (other sites)?
  - Are there additional connections to Web search engines and subject trees?

Information: What?
- Content:
  - What is the breadth and depth of information provided?
  - Are documentation and citations provided?
  - What is the reading/comprehension level?
  - Is it thorough and accurate?
  - Does it provides information not available elsewhere?
- Organization:
  - Is it clearly labeled and organized?
  - Is it useful for curriculum and personal interest?
  - Are the format and conventions used appropriate for the content?

Presentation: Wow?
- Access:
  - What is the load time?
  - Is there a text-only option?
- Design:
  - Are text and graphics well balanced?
  - Production elements: typestyles, background, page layout?
  - Artistic elements: function or decorative?
  - Glitz factor? Do the bells and whistles outweigh the content?
- Language: Spelling, grammar, composition?

Sample Links Activity: Pathfinder Checklist

For this project, students are required to keep a working checklist of all the resources they have used throughout the project. They will submit a formal bibliography with each unit report, citing the resources used for that particular subtopic. The Pathfinder will be kept in their folders for the extent of the project as a resource guide. Students previously have used both the Pathfinder and Citation worksheets. For this activity, both librarian and teacher act as instructors; the class is divided into two groups to make the library "tour" more manageable.

Activity Plan:

Focus:

    A. Identify and locate possible resources for country information.

    B. Record information about resources recommended and used.

Links/Logistics:

    A. Prior knowledge/skills:

        Student knowledge of general library layout

        Student knowledge of generic reference tools

        Previous experience using Citation worksheets

    B. Materials needed:

        1. Pathfinder worksheet (library map on front; resource list on back)

        2. Citation worksheets (fill-in-the-blank forms for different resource formats)

    C. Facility set-up: normal library facility plus blackboard

    D. Time constraints: one 40-minute period

Input/Implementation:

    A. Whole group

        1. "Good travelers always use a map to help them locate the places they need to find. Today we're going to take you on a mini-tour of the library, pointing out resources you will need to use for your own investigations. What kind of landmarks do you think we might need to visit?"

        2. Discuss and note on the board class suggestions of various information sources.

Distribute Pathfinder worksheets. Explain that the groups will go in different directions, but will cover all the highlights. Tell students that this is their first scouting expedition to locate possible resources to use in their own research. Remind students to note call numbers and locations on their Pathfinders, so that they can find those resources later.

    B. Separate groups

        1. Walk groups around the library to available resources, briefly discussing the features and access points of each.

        2. Have students write likely titles to use and their call numbers or locations on their worksheets.

PATHFINDER GUIDE FOR RESEARCH ON:

_____

search terms (key words) to use:

_____ _____ _____ _____ _____

_____ _____ _____ _____ _____

suggested resources: **call numbers / location:**

A. BASIC INFORMATION AND OVERVIEW:

General encyclopedias: _____

Special encylopedias: _____

Dictionaries: _____

Almanacs: _____

Atlas: _____

B. MORE DETAILED INFORMATION:

Books about subject: _____

Books about related subjects: _____

Multi-media formats, including CD-ROMs: _____

Online databases: _____

C. INFORMATION ABOUT RECENT EVENTS:

Readers' Guide to Periodical Literature: _____

Magazine Article Summaries: _____

ADDITIONAL RESOURCES: **source:**

Internet sites: _____

Broadcasts (radio/television):   _____

Community Resources: _____

Personal interviews: _____

Reproducible from _FLIP IT! An Information Skills Strategy for Student Researchers_ by Alice H. Yucht (1997, Linworth Publishing, Inc.)

Figure 2.2 Pathfinder Worksheet

CITATIONS of RESOURCES USED
Multi-volume Resource (encyclopedias, etc.)

_____

_____ sub-topic

_____,_____. " _____.
Author's name (if given): last name first.   Title of article (in quotation marks).

_____.   _____,_____.
Name of encyclopedia (underlined).   Publishing company, copyright date.

_____,_____.
volume, page(s).

- -

_____ sub-topic

_____,_____. " _____.
Author's name (if given): last name first.   Title of article (in quotation marks).

_____.   _____,_____.
Name of encyclopedia (underlined).   Publishing company, copyright date.

_____,_____.
volume, page(s).

- -

_____ sub-topic

_____,_____. " _____.
Author's name (if given): last name first.   Title of article (in quotation marks).

_____.   _____,_____.
Name of encyclopedia (underlined).   Publishing company, copyright date.

_____,_____.
volume, page(s).

- -

_____ sub-topic

_____,_____. " _____.
Author's name (if given): last name first.   Title of article (in quotation marks).

_____.   _____,_____.
Name of encyclopedia (underlined).   Publishing company, copyright date.

_____,_____.
volume, page(s).

- -

Figure 2.3 Citation Worksheet

3. Demonstrate electronic resources if time permits.
4. Explain that detailed instructions on specific resources will occur later; this is just "window-shopping" to see what is available.
5. After the tour is completed, have the group brainstorm possible search words to use for the subtopics they will be investigating.

C. Whole group
1. Discuss possible resources in the community.
2. Brainstorm ways to access these resources.
3. Distribute Citation worksheets for both single-volume and multi-volume resources.

Product/Proof:

A. Give students five minutes to locate and record on the Citation worksheets one single-volume and one multi-volume resource they think will be useful.
B. Observe and evaluate their choices, supervising and assisting as needed.
C. Students will use their Pathfinders as resource guides for all of the research necessary for this project.

Input Activities

Input is the most labor-intensive stage of the process, as students implement the information to develop a workable solution. As with every stage of this process, the two foundation questions that underscore all the strategies:

What do I already know that will help me? and

What focus do I need to keep in mind?

will keep searchers on task as they acquire and implement the information they have accessed.

Specific concerns now include:

- What kinds of information do I need to use? Why?
- How can I best record and acknowledge what I have found?
- How should I prioritize, categorize, and organize what I have just learned?
- Do I have all the information necessary or are other details needed to make sense of what I now have?
- What inferences can I make? What new ideas do I now have to consider?

Input skills include all the traditional literature appreciation activities, as students interact with all kinds of formats and genres. Explaining what defines a picture book is a focus unit; learning how to locate picture books by author's last name would involve links activities; but reading and discussing a specific book involves INPUT from both teacher and student. Input skills units include:

- Acquiring information (Note: "Conventions" refer to standard design elements.)
  - Print conventions and formats
  - Electronic conventions and formats
  - Personal conventions and formats
  - Taking notes
  - Understanding visuals, such as maps, charts, and graphs
  - Citing sources
- Evaluating information
  - Authority and currency
  - Fact vs. opinion
  - Primary vs. secondary sources
  - Comparing and contrasting
- Integrating information from a variety of sources
- Organizing information
  - Informational frameworks:
    - Categories of information
    - Arrangements of information
    - Patterns of information use
  - Identifying topics and subtopics
  - Outlines
  - Graphic organizers
  - Diagramming and webbing

In some cases, these skills may overlap or repeat focus skills, but go into greater detail depending upon their use and application. Obviously, many of these skill strategies will be used simultaneously as students examine and evaluate the information.

Sample Input Activity: Note Taking

This research assignment focuses on the economics of each country. Students will be using a four-box worksheet format (see sample worksheet) to record and cite information.

To prepare the worksheet:

> Fold an 8.5 x 11-inch paper in half vertically, then in half horizontally to form four boxes.
>
> Label the top left box FOCUS, the top right box LOOKED UP IN, and the two bottom boxes IMPORTANT POINTS.

This unit uses several input skills, such as using print conventions to identify information, taking notes, citing sources, and integrating and evaluating information from several sources.

Activity plan:

Focus: Gather and record information about the economics of a country.

Links/Logistics:

- Prior knowledge/skills:
    - Understanding of standard terms and concepts used to describe a country's economy
    - Experience using basic reference sources
    - Experience taking notes using only key words and phrases
    - Experience writing simple bibliographic citations
    - Previous use of four-box worksheet for taking notes
- Materials needed:
    - four-box notetaking worksheets (can be prepared in advance in the classroom, as part of a pre-search FOCUS activity)
    - Pathfinder and Citation worksheets (in students' project folders)
    - Library collection
- Facility set-up: normal library workspace plus blackboard
- Time constraints: one 40-minute period plus extra individual time, as needed

Input/Implementation:

- (Note: This step could be done before coming to the library.) Discuss possible search terms for information about economics of their country. Record these key words on the blackboard. Discuss related terminology that might be used to find information (e.g. monetary = money, basic unit, coins, bills). Terms used as FOCUS words should include: monetary system, agricultural products, manufacturing products, and transportation. (This activity could be done with Focus Frames worksheet in class.) Have students list the chosen FOCUS terms in the FOCUS box, labeled alphabetically.
- Discuss likely resources for this kind of information. List resource formats to be used in LOOKED UP IN box, labeled with symbols (star, circle).

4-BOX NOTE TAKING WORKSHEET

COUNTRY:_____TOPIC:_____

FOCUS:

A. money system

B. agricultural products

C. industries/manufacturing

D. transportation systems

E. employment opportunities

LOOKED UP IN:

*   encyclopedia

almanac

@   land and people

$ book title:

IMPORTANT POINTS:

1.

2.

3.

4.

5.

6.

7.

8.

9.

10.

Figure 2.4 4-Box Note Taking Worksheet

- Have each student find the encyclopedia article they listed previously on their multi-volume Citation worksheet. Make sure students have recorded all necessary information for their citation.
- Briefly discuss and review the arrangement/conventions of encyclopedia use (linking to previous lessons and use). Have students find information about their country's money system in the encylopedia article, and record the information as Number 1 in the IMPORTANT POINTS box. Use this fact to demonstrate how to record the information in brief format , and then to indicate FOCUS letter and LOOKED UP IN symbol in parentheses next to the fact.

  Example: Shekel is basic unit (B *).
- Have students find and record a list of agricultural products, with topic and resource symbols.
- Repeat this process with another source, such as a specialized encyclopedia or an almanac, until students have gathered at least one set of facts for each focus topic. (Students can quickly see which subtopics need more information. Since they are writing facts in only brief words or phrases, they also are learning how to extract rather than copy information from a source.)
- Make sure that students are finding information for each subtopic, that they are writing only words or phrases, and that they are noting the subtopic and source for each entry.

Product/Proof:
- Check students' worksheets for completeness, accuracy, and correct form.
- Students will use this information to prepare their report to the Territorial Commissioner.

Payoff Activities

Payoff or presentation skills have been given little attention in traditional Library Skills curricula. We have usually helped students find the information, without paying much attention to how the results will be presented. We have assumed the reason for the information search (e.g. a teacher-assigned project) determined the format for the final product.

New technology has changed the range of possible information formats, and there is greater emphasis on designing end-products for authentic assessment of student learning. As the information literacy experts, we have also become the presentation/product format consultants, helping teachers design more innovative ways for students to demonstrate their knowledge.

No matter what the final product looks or sounds like, it must answer the following questions:

Have I effectively answered my FOCUS questions?

Do I have an acceptable solution to my original problem?

What kind of product is required? How do I produce what is asked for?

Have I proved my ability to demonstrate my new understanding?

What kind of "profit" can I earn from these efforts?

What additional possibilities might I now consider?

Payoff skills most clearly reflect both internal and external evaluation of the entire process based on the end-result. Have students demonstrated:

- integration of prior and new knowledge
- ability to effectively and independently use new skills
- efficient time on task
- consistent use of higher-order thinking skills
- self-motivation, and
- striving for excellence

throughout the activity, or have they coasted, doing as little as possible? Evaluation of these factors will determine the final payoff: the students' satisfaction with the work accomplished, and the "merit pay" received from the teacher.

Payoff skills units could include:

- Kind of product or format needed

    Format possibilities:

    Print

    Multi-media

    Electronic

    Artifacts

    Personal

- Production requirements

    Format constraints

    Scope and purpose of product

- "Repackaging" Concerns and Considerations

    Copyright issues

    Point of view

    Creativity vs. clarity

- Organization of information
- Documentation of sources used
- Evaluation of results

Sample Payoff Activity:
Preparing a Bibliography

Students have been recording bibliographic information on the various
Citation worksheets (see Links Activity) for each resource they have used.
They need to submit a unit bibliography with each report, as well as a comprehensive bibliography at the end of the project. The final production of the
bibliography will take place in the computer lab as part of a combined lesson
on databases and word processing. This activity will be completed after the
first unit's research time; subsequent bibliography production may require
only brief review sessions.

Activity Plan:
Focus: Creating a formal bibliography
Links/Logistics:
- Prior knowledge/skills:
    Student knowledge of purpose of bibliographies
    Student knowledge of and experience with requirements of
        bibliographic citations (resource format worksheets)
- Materials needed:
    Students' Citation worksheets (from project folders)
    Demonstration entries (postercards) for each resource format
    3x5 index cards or similar scrap paper
    masking tape
    Bibliography format study guide
- Facility set-up: classroom style
- Time constraints: one 40-minute period

Input/Implementation:
- Review and discuss the purpose of bibliographies. Point out the wall
  poster: "Give Credit where it's due: Cite the Site where you Sighted
  your facts.") (See appendix.)
- Ask the class how many resources they used for this particular unit.
  Have them find specific entries for this unit on their Citation worksheets (should be noted as a subtopic on the top line of each entry
  on the worksheets), and put these sheets in front of them on the
  desk.
- Display demonstration entries for single-volume and multi-volume
  resources. Ask the class to point out similarities and differences in
  format and punctuation between the entries. Compare other entries
  for resource formats used in this unit.
- Have students check their own entries on their worksheets for correct format and punctuation.
- Distribute index cards or scrap paper.
- Explain that students are going to copy each entry from their worksheets to a card; carefully following the worksheet/demo format and
  punctuation.

- Explain the hanging indent format as an "upside down paragraph": the first word of the first line begins at the left margin, and everything else is indented on left. Explain that if there is a blank space in the worksheet entry (e.g., no author), they should start at the margin with the next word in the entry.
- Remind students to put a check mark in the upper left corner of the worksheet entry after they have copied it onto a card, so they don't duplicate entries. After all entries from the worksheets have been copied onto cards, the worksheets should be put in the project folders, leaving only the cards on the desk.
- Display all demonstration entries. Explain that they need to be put in some kind of order for the final bibliography to be produced. Discuss possibilities. Explain why it doesn't matter where the information came from as long as the source is cited.
- Point out that the first word in the entry (located at the left margin) will be used for alphabetizing these citations into one list.
- Have the class rearrange the demo entries into alphabetical order by author (or title, if there is no author). Have students hold postercards and line up in front of the group.
- Have students arrange their own cards in order (top to bottom) on the desk, and check each other for accuracy.
- Have students tape the cards in order (daisy chain) for final production in the computer lab.
- Distribute the Bibliography format study guide as a review sheet to be kept in the project folders.

Product/Proof:

- In the computer lab, students will use their cards to enter information into a master database of resources used. They will then transfer the information into a word processing document so they can format and print the bibliography to accompany the unit report to the territorial commissioner.
- The cards and final bibliography will be evaluated for completeness and accuracy of information and formatting.

<u>Notes</u>

Chapter 3

Input: Implementing Resource-based Learning

Integrating Content and Process

"If students are to succeed in the 21st century and meet the future's challenge:

- They must recognize the importance of education as a lifelong effort.
- They will need to communicate effectively with others through reading, writing, speaking, computing, the arts, and technology.
- They will need to respect and understand people of diverse backgrounds in our diverse society.
- They will need to understand environmental and other issues with worldwide implications.
- They will need to make informed decisions for themselves, their families, their communities and our country.
- They will need to contribute to our society.
- They will need to take responsibility for their own behavior."

(Massachusetts Department of Education.
Charting the Course: the common chapters)

Regardless of the subject or grade level, curricular and instructional design is constructed of two intermeshed strands:

- Content — the "what" of the course, including
    - fundamental concepts, theories, questions, and sub-topics
    - points of view and/or frames of reference
    - materials to be used for information delivery
- Process — the "how" of the course, including
    - skills necessary for information acquisition, comprehension and development
    - inquiry and experiential strategies and techniques
    - activity protocols
    - assessment rubrics

Acquiring and applying knowledge in any subject area requires integrating the new information with the learner's prior knowledge. Some of what is learned may be subject-specific, while some knowledge becomes part of lifetime learning strategies we now call information literacy.

Textbooks and teacher as the only sources of information in a classroom are no longer enough to maintain a student's interest. Students today are accustomed to many kinds of information formats, from picture books to Web pages. If we are to prepare students to be effective adults, we must help them develop their critical and creative thinking skills in a variety of activities, appealing to multiple intelligences and learning styles. Students' natural curiosity about the world beyond the classroom can be fostered through exposure to the wide variety of resources available in our ever-expanding information universe.

Contemporary learning theory underscores the importance of students' developing information expertise. Cognitive psychology recommends inquiry as the best learning process. Students construct meaning through continued developmental interaction with a wide range of information resources and application problems.

"Resource-based Learning" is the term now used for an educational model that actively involves students in the meaningful use of print, non-print, and human resources. The school library program is a basic component of the model by:

- providing resources and information beyond the textbook. Materials reflect the diversity of students' abilities, aptitudes, interests, and backgrounds.
- offering instruction in information skills to access, evaluate, use and construct information in a variety of formats. These generic skills are useful for content in all areas of interest.
- furnishing a central resource facility to all members of the educational community, with a collection that meets the needs of all learners. Materials may be used within the library, accessed electronically, or borrowed for use elsewhere.

As the facilitator who connects students and teachers with both content and skills, the school librarian's roles as information specialist, teacher, and instructional consultant become more integral to the learning process.

Collaborative Planning

Remember the activities in the world geography project discussed previously to demonstrate different kinds of information skills strategies? For 15 years the students had been doing traditional "country reports"—dull duplications of basic information, culminating in an international festival focused on food. The teacher dreaded having to read and grade the reports every year, but had attempted only minor variations in report format. Even the parents and students were bored with the same old thing. Meanwhile, the real world offered new technologies for information access, input, and output. There were more students from other cultures and lifestyles to be assimilated into this school's culture. There were more real-world travel options for students and their families, and even more discussion and depiction of travel beyond the earth's boundaries. It was time for a change, and as the new librarian, I was the catalyst.

The social studies teacher mentioned the annual project at the beginning of the school year and said she hoped I might know of some new resources to use. I suggested we meet to discuss the project and look at some of the recently- purchased materials. At our first meeting, I took notes, using a FLIP IT! Activity Planning Guide. I demonstrated some of the possibilities available with Internet access, which was new to the school. We discussed the research skills the students already had, and I noted areas needing review or development. Finally, I asked what curricular involvement the other subject teachers had in this grade-level project. "Not much," she replied. "since it's mostly a social studies assignment. Can you suggest ways to tie in the other subjects?"

That first year our theme was "arrivals from America." Students were told, "Your family is being transferred to _____. Your parents are busy packing and taking care of paperwork and travel details. As the oldest child, you are in charge of finding the basic information about living and working in this different country, so you and the rest of your family do not embarrass yourselves while you are there." Unit reports took the form of letters to former classmates, comparing life in this new place with familiar experiences in America. Students needed to evaluate and synthesize the facts they found, showing similarities and differences between the two cultures. In Language Arts, students read essays written by other famous travelers as models for developing their own material into informative and interesting narratives. Food-tasting became a weekly opportunity to learn about different cultures. Final exhibition was still primarily a show-and-tell of clothing and travel souvenirs, but even that had a new viewpoint as the students described their "foreign sojourns."

The latest version of this interdisciplinary project was shaped by ideas from movies and television shows like Star Trek and Third Rock from the Sun . Students now look forward to doing research because they actually get to use their knowledge in many different ways. Assignments and reports are much more interesting to read, and easier to evaluate, as teachers find themselves looking forward to discovering what new twists and innovations the students will produce. The entire grade-level team meets during an inservice day to plan the details, and additional ideas and possibilities are "deposited" with the librarian as project coordinator for discussion at faculty meetings. The complete file of planning guides, handouts, activity outlines, assignment details, report formats, ideas in progress, and schedules fills a two-inch binder on each teacher's desk. Enthusiasm and interest in such projects—and in the unlimited possibilities of such resource-based learning activities—has dramatically increased the library's involvement in curricular planning.

FLIP IT! works particularly well as a framework for developing collaborative resource-based activities by outlining the interrelationships of the skills and information that will be used in order to complete the project. Using this kind of form to gather and organize input from both the teacher and the librarian helps ensure that:

- necessary library and subject skills and content will be introduced, reinforced, or reviewed, as needed,
- ample and appropriate resources are available,
- teacher and librarian have clearly defined roles and responsibilities for each element of the project,
- strategies for critical thinking are an integral part of the learning activities,

- students will have a clear understanding of what is expected of them, and
- timeframes will be established and scheduled as needed.

These working guides serve as both reminder and outline for the librarian and the teacher, specifying the activities or requirements involved at each stage of the process. I recommend using this form as a notetaking guide as soon as a teacher mentions scheduling any library activity, even though revisions will be needed throughout the planning process. When dealing with teachers who balk at planning in advance, I explain that this paperwork is necessary to "document the library's program and statistics for administrative reports."

Discussing projects in advance with teachers and being part of the total planning process is the ideal way to ensure that resource-based activities will require more than copying of information. The best way to suggest alternatives to standard report formats is by showing teachers that:

- when students have to "restructure" and "repackage" the information they have acquired, they will be forced to think more critically and creatively,
- a variety of format possibilities engenders more enthusiasm for the project,
- "authentic" presentations offer greater understanding of real-life skills,
- collaborative planning increases the likelihood of student success with the assignment, and
- carefully planned and designed project requirements make assessment easier.

Planning together means that both teacher and librarian have an equal stake in the process and the final product. Working together also reinforces the librarian's role in the total educational program. This is an important issue for program advocacy, especially as we hear more about how Internet access will eliminate the need for school libraries and librarians. Few teachers have the time to keep up with all the new resources that could be used to complement and extend their curriculum's content. Nor will most teachers develop the "information navigation" expertise that librarians must maintain as part of their professional responsibilities.

Collaborative planning is beneficial for demonstrating the role of the library program in the total educational infrastructure.

- Librarians can demonstrate the value of lifelong learning skills to both students and other adults. Since information resource formats change so quickly, we must continue to learn to master the new technology skills needed.
- Teachers view librarians as equal instructional partners, and parents see that librarians are professional educators.
- Success breeds success. One joint effort usually leads to more possibilities as other teachers notice the results of these cooperative ventures.
- Administrators see more value in the library budget; expensive

LIBRARY ACTIVITY PLANNING GUIDE

Teacher: _____ **Subject:** _____ **date:** _____

FOCUS: (specifying)

Students will be investigating:

> **TOPIC(s):**

>> **as part of Unit of Study on:**

> **Rationale:**

LINKS/LOGISTICS: (strategizing)

A. Prior knowledge/skills students should have:

> **Content:**

> **Process:**

B. Resources:

> **Recommendations:**

> **Restrictions:**

C. Constraints: e.g. time, facilities, student abilities

INPUT/IMPLEMENTATION: (searching, sorting, sifting, storing)

Content:

> **Kinds of information needed:**

Process:

> **Library/Information Skills:**

> **Thinking/Writing Activities:**

PRODUCT/PROOF: (sharing)

Product Format: **Product Requirements:**

Assignment timeline: DATES:

Introduction:	_____ **in class**	_____ **in library**
Library Work:	_____ **search strategies**	_____ **notetaking**
Due Dates:	_____ **notes**	_____ **work in progress**
		_____ **related activities**
	_____ **bibliography**	_____ **final product**

Figure 3.1 Library Activity Planning Guide

resources are being used more, justifying their cost. Increased collection use as a result of greater curricular involvement is the best way to substantiate requests for additional budget funds.

Explanation of Specifics in Planning Guide

Teacher: Subject: Date: discussed and agreed upon
Make copies for both teacher and librarian, so there are no surprises later.

FOCUS: (specifying)
Students will be investigating:
>   TOPIC(s):
>>   as part of Unit of Study on:
Does the library have enough material available and appropriate for this grade-level?
>   number of students working on project
>   depth of information needed
>   types of information needed
>   Rationale: reason for activity, desired student behavioral outcomes

LINKS/LOGISTICS: (strategizing)
A. Prior knowledge/skills students should have:
>   Content:
>>   What terms are students familiar with from classwork?
>>   What subtopics, descriptors, and subject headings does the teacher recommend?
>>   What other terms or descriptors are used by resource materials for this topic?
>>   How much do students already know about this topic?
>>   How much do students already know about using the necessary resources?
>   Process:
>>   What skills will students need to use?
>>   What skills does the teacher assume that students already have mastered? Why?
B. Resources:
>   Recommendations:
>>   What resources does the teacher expect to be available?
>>   What other resources does the librarian think are appropriate?
>>   What else might be needed? Why?
>   Restrictions:
>>   What does the teacher or librarian want students NOT to use? Why?
>>   How will restrictions be handled or reinforced?
C. Constraints:
>>   What is the consideration of diversity of learning abilities and learning styles in this class?

STUDENT'S RESEARCH ACTIVITY GUIDE

FOCUS: (specifying)

    A. Essential questions I need to answer:

    B. Definitions and terms I will need to know:

LINKS : (strategizing)

    A. Keywords to use:

    B. Related topics to consider:

    C. Special resources to investigate:

        Pathfinder available?

    D. Other possible connections:

INPUT: (searching, sorting, sifting, storing)

A. Kinds of Information needed:

    content:

    citations:

B. Procedures/paperwork needed:

    — notetaking formats

    — computer access?

    — other considerations

PRODUCT/PROOF: (sharing)

Product Format: Product Requirements:

— see teacher's assignment sheet   — see teacher's grading rubrics

Assignment Timeline: Dates:

Introduction:	_____ in class	_____ in library
Library Work:	_____ search strategies	_____ notetaking
Due Dates:	_____ notes	_____ work in progress
		_____ related activities
	_____ bibliography	_____ final product

Worth ?? of total grade:

Reproducible from *FLIP IT! An Information Skills Strategy for Student Researchers* by Alice H. Yucht (1997, Linworth Publishing, Inc.)

Figure 3.2 Student's Research Activity Guide

How much time is needed and/or available:
> for coverage of subject content?
> for pre-search (including skills instruction), research, post-
> search activities?
> in the classroom? in the library?

What other facilities or set-ups are needed? (computer lab, art room,
printing, display)

INPUT/IMPLEMENTATION: (searching, sorting, sifting, storing)
Content:
> Kinds of Information Needed:
> How much detail or depth is expected of students? Why?
> What additional formats might be required?

Process:
> Library/Information Skills:
>> What specific skills and materials will need to be introduced,
>> developed, or reviewed?
>> Delivery format? Context , strategies, and activities necessary?
>> Time constraints? Support/supervision/evaluation necessary?
> Thinking/writing Activities:
>> Note-taking procedures and formats to be used?
>> Context, strategies, and activities necessary?
>> Materials needed? Provided by?

PRODUCT/PROOF: (shar+-ing)
Product Format: Product Requirements:
> Examples? Possibilities? Reasons for choice?
> Assessment rubrics and grading concerns? Provided by whom? When?

Assignment Timeline: Dates: as part of master calendar?
Introduction: _____ in class   _____ in library
> By whom? How?
Library Work: _____ search strategies   _____ notetaking
> Forms to follow? checkpoints for additional help needed?
Due Dates: _____ notes   _____ work in progress
                                          _____ related activities
> _____ bibliography   _____ final product
> Evaluation concerns? Publishing/presentation/display
> possibilities?

Product and Presentation Formats

Reports that look like poorly rewritten encyclopedia articles are common because that is what too many students think research should look like—dry, static regurgitation of data. Most print formats (encyclopedias, newspapers, magazines, and books) deliver the information in carefully structured recitations of facts. If that is the only model students have for research end-products, that is what they will produce. That is also the reason we constantly are contending with plagiarism. Students don't think they can write more effectively than the authors of those resources. Unless we insist that students use more creativity to demonstrate understanding and application of the new information they have acquired, we will continue to be faced with the same boring results.

As librarians and information managers, we have a unique expertise that we often forget to use—we are used to coping with many different information formats for a variety of purposes. We need to use that expertise and knowledge to

- teach students how to extract and produce information in many different ways, and
- help teachers design more innovative report formats that demonstrate authentic learning.

Look around the library. You have posters, picture books, charts, realia, and multimedia, all conveying information in different ways. Look around your life. What about memos, letters, official documents, newspapers and magazines, junk mail, program guides, and even post-it notes? And those are just the print versions!

In today's "info-glut" world, we need to teach our students to become effective information producers, and we can't do that by accepting the same old report formats. But we can't just say "design something unique." We have to demonstrate how and why different formats work, and provide many different examples. We cannot expect students to aim for a bullseye if they don't know what the target looks like. So we also need to teach information literacy in all kinds of presentation and production formats. With the ease and availability of today's technology, students have an extensive variety of information "re-packaging" options. Of course, this also means a renewed emphasis on both print and electronic rights and responsibilities, or why a student's report cannot be just a collection of reproductions or a set of hypertext links to the original sources. Re-packaging means re-thinking, re-filtering, and re-constructing, not just re-organizing.

When faced with any assignment, students invariably ask the same two questions:

- How long does it have to be?
- How is it going to be graded?

I have found that making assignments tighter (e.g. shorter, broken into smaller pieces of a whole, or even just much more specific in requirements) helps keep students focused. There is nothing wrong with brevity, as long as everything important is covered.

Generic Grading Rubric

This generic grading/evaluation rubric is useful for any format:

Focus:

Demonstrates a clear understanding of the issue	10 points
Provides answers to the target questions	25 points

Logistics:

Presents information in an organized and logical order,
in a way that makes sense to the reader/viewer, including:

Introduction/attention-grabber	5 points
Development of important details	5 points
Conclusion/summary	5 points

Information Content:

Demonstrates use of a variety of resources and viewpoints	5 points
Answers the target questions with specific facts and supporting details	10 points
Is both meaningful and interesting to other readers/viewers	5 points
Presents accurate and documented information	10 points

Presentation:

Meets recognized standards of writing and presentation mechanics	10 points
Identifies and credits other authors when their work is quoted	5 points
Presentation methods are relevant and appropriate to content	5 points

IT: Innovative thinking

Extra credit for creativity above and beyond the requirements, but still relevant to the intent of the assignment	10 points

Generic Report Formats

The following formats have been used successfully in grades 4 through 12. Because the information required is clearly defined, has a specific place in the final product, and has a genuine reason for being included, students are often more comfortable tackling these kinds of assignments.

Display format. Biography cards (actually poster-sized, but based on baseball cards).

Focus: Graphic organizer for presenting most important information about an individual

Layout:

Front of the card:
Portrait or symbol of individual
Timeline border of important events in personal life

Back of the card:
Bulleted list of accomplishments
Brief paragraph explaining reason(s) for fame
Bibliography of resources used

Input: Can be as detailed or simple as appropriate for the grade level.
Sample topics might include:

Explorers	Scientists and Inventors
Notable Women	Unsung Heroes
Native Americans	Famous Immigrants
Desperados and Daredevils	Musicians, Artists, or Writers
Presidential Wannabes	Person of the Year or Decade

Presentation:

Posterboard cards can be placed on easels, hung from ceiling grids, or used as sandwich boards in a parade.

Smaller versions can be produced on file folders, as open folder with information on facing inside panels, or stood up as tent display with information on the outside panels.

Sample Student Assignment Guide
for Biography Card

Subject: World History   Topic: Age of Exploration

Focus: European explorers and navigators, 1300 - 1600

Logistics:
    Resources: minimum of three different resources, including
       only one general encylcopedic source
    Due on: _____(date)
    Worth: 20% of total marking period grade

Information Needed:
    Who/When: name of explorer
                     Personal life
                     Education and training
    Where/What: Places and routes of exploration
                     Problems encountered
    How/Why: Political involvements/sponsorships
                     Effects of exploration

Product: Posterboard "baseball card" format, with:
    Side 1: Portrait/symbol of explorer
           Map of exploration routes
           Timeline border showing datesand places explored
    Side 2: Full name; with boxed "stats" on:
             biographical information
             geographical explorations
             political connections
             effects of exploration
         Resources used (bibliography)

Print Format: Facts in Brief Sheet.

Focus: Single page report, with important details about a topic in bulleted categories.

>   Facts in Brief sheets can used as mini-reports, study guides, oral presentation prompts, or unit outlines.

Layout: This format is used for the final product, not for notetaking because students will need to "restructure,"—categorize, prioritize, and re-organize the information to be included.

Information Categories:

Focus: A brief explanation of the main idea (30-50 words). Since this is the topic/summary statement, it should be written after students have completed all of the research.

Links:

>   Related topics (and how and why they are related). Connections to larger unit of study and other relevant topics or subjects. Students may not need to report on these topics, but they should be able to explain the connections.

>   Resources used. Documentation to show that the student didn't just skim the textbook or make up the facts. (This could be put on the back of the page or on a separate page.)

Input: Important Details:

>   The five most important facts about the topic (the lead sentences for each paragraph of a full report).

>   Terms/concepts: definitions, explanations, and additional details necessary for understanding.

Payoff: Reasons for Posterity:

>   knowledge of this topic provides greater understanding of and additional...

>   Possibilities and applications.

Sample Facts in Brief Sheet

Subject: Submarines   Unit of Study: Transportation Technology

Focus: Submarines are self-contained vehicles used to travel underwater.
Most modern submarines have long, cigar-shaped bodies, enabling them to
travel swiftly and easily through the water. Submarines are used primarily
or scientific research and military warfare.

Links:
- Oceanography
- Jacques Cousteau
- Woods Hole Scientific Institute (Maine)
- Naval warfare attack submarines
- Surveillance submarines
- Periscope
- Twenty Thousand Leagues Under the Sea by Jules Verne

Important Details:
- First workable submarine built 1620 by Dutch scientist named Cornelius von Drebbel.
- Submarines have been an important part of military tactics since the Civil War.
- Basic parts and interior arrangement of submarine types
- Submarines can be powered by variety of fuels and power generators.
- Submarines can stay underwater for extended periods of time.

Payoffs:
- Unique form of vehicle for a variety of uses
- Submarine design as an influence on spaceship design

Performance Format: Mini-Videos. Television programming packs a lot of information into time-specific segments. Students quickly see the possibilities of this format for all kinds of demonstrations, multi-media presentations, and docu-dramas. This format is excellent for developing and strengthening communication and teamwork skills. Still, it is not as easy as it first seems because working within a specific presentation timeframe means that every second must count.

Focus:
- Topic selection and rationale for choice of production format
- Specific skills required
- Performance format

Logistics:
- Production timetable
- Materials, set-up needed
- Sequence of presentation
- Timing and/or space requirements of each presentation element

Input:
- Key points to be made
- Main idea and supporting details, coherently and cogently presented
- Techniques to keep audience interested and involved

Payoff:
- Summary, final persuasive pitch
- Why this information is important

Sample Production Guide for "You Are There" Video Series

Focus:
- "Milestones of Technology" videos — student productions
- Specific skills required
  scriptwriters
  crafts: costume and prop makers, scenery builders
  stage manager/director
  actors
  videographer
- Performance format: docu-drama—five- to eight-minute mini-play

Logistics:
- Production timetable
  research: 1 week
  script and craft production: 1 week
  rehearsal and filming: 2 days
- Materials, set-up needed
  TV studio schedule
  see individual scripts for crafts needed
- Sequence of Presentation
  Opening: program logo, voice-over, dissolve to
  reporter's introduction, setting the scene
  dramatic events of discovery
  reporter's wrap-up: importance of discovery or event
  voice-over during montage of results of discovery
  program logo, coming attractions, credits
- Timing and/or space requirements of each presentation element:
  see scripts

Input:
- Key points to be demonstrated:
  Who: Scientists involved
  When, Where: Time period, lab conditions
  How, What: Process of discovery and/or invention
  Why, Wow: Results of this new technological development
- Production style and techniques to be used: see individual scripts

Payoffs:
- Cooperative learning activities; entire production is team effort
- Knowledge of video production: formats, techniques, equipment
- Broader knowledge of history and development of technology
- Educational product for teachers to use with other classes

Written or Oral Format: Book Review/Report. Rather than a simple recital of the plot details, this framework requires more critical thinking, and requires the reviewer to examine both the content and process of the product.

Focus: What this book is really about:
- Basic theme or subject of the book
- Main characters and their problem(s), and/or
- Issues to be resolved or examined

Layout: How the text of the book is structured:
- Arrangement, organization, layout
- Fiction
    Standard genre characteristics used
    Plot summary (no more than five key events)
    Literary form used
- Nonfiction
    What kind of pictures, if any, are there?
    Chapters? Table of Contents? Index ?
    Authority, bibliography of resources used?
- Point of view
- Packaging details
    Cover illustration
    Size/format of publication

Impact: What makes this particular book so interesting?
- Unusual ideas, setting, or subject
- Personal reactions
- New things you learned from this book

Passing It On: Who else would be interested in this book? Why?
- Other books on this topic, in this series, by this author.
- How you would rate this book? For example, is it:
    a six-shiver mystery?
    a four-handkerchief sob story?
    a 20/20 exclusive?
    a newsflash headline?

Other Product Examples
SUBJECT: Language Arts

PRODUCT: Book Report — Problem Novel   FORMAT: 3-D Display

FOCUS: Character analysis:
        "School Locker" (using a shoebox) for a lead character from a novel

LINKS: School locker structure and likely contents
        Personal artifacts as character identification

INPUT: Information gleaned from text of novel regarding the character's
    interests, physical appearance, and everyday life

PRESENTATION:
        "Locker" will include items (miniatures, samples, and notes) repre-
            senting different aspects of character's life, problems, and interests.

SUBJECT: Science — Solar System

PRODUCT: Planetary Postcards   FORMAT: Display

FOCUS: Information about specific planets
      Space explorers send postcards home to earth.

LINKS: Important elements defining planets as ecosystems
      Postcard format: picture on one side; information on the other side

INPUT: Details about each planet's physical characteristics

PRESENTATION:
      Side 1: colorful drawing of planet
      Side 2: Message "home" — two paragraphs:
         1. What planet looks like to visitor
         2. Problems encountered while traveling to/landing on planet

SUBJECT: American History

PRODUCT: Application for Land Grant   FORMAT: Written

FOCUS: Settling of the West
        Paperwork for family homestead

LINKS: Reasons for westward migration
        Territorial conditions
        Ethnic groups as immigrants
        Primary vs. secondary sources
INPUT: Routes across America taken by immigrants
        Governmental regulations (local, regional)
        Geographic and climatic conditions
        Skills and resources needed to establish homesteads
        Family histories and artifacts

PRESENTATION: Paperwork should include:
        Birth certificates, travel documents and other realia
        Map of area, with homestead boundaries
        Physical description of homestead, with details for use of land
        Invoices for equipment and/or loans needed
        Letters of reference from neighbors, officials, and others

SUBJECTS: Interdisciplinary: Geography, Math, Technology, Art

PRODUCT: Giant Countries   FORMAT: Display

FOCUS: Floor maps (48" square) of individual countries, showing
      physical topography
      political divisions
      major tourist sites

LINKS: Social Studies: map skills
      Technology:
          visual technology**
          construction diagrams
      Mathematics: measurement, scale and proportion
         Art: spatial concepts
            calligraphy and graphics design
            painting and construction techniques

INPUT natural topography of country
      cities and provinces
      major transportation routes
      tourism and travel issues

PRESENTATION:
      Worldwide display on floor of all-purpose room exhibition with each
        country:
          in continental arrangement
          aligned with border countries
          displaying three-dimensional models of
            significant landforms
            tourist attractions

**Students use overhead projectors to enlarge map templates from 8"x11" blackline masters to 48"
square blank paper for floor maps. In math class, they calculate the comparative scale and proportions; in art class, they paint the maps, label the important sites, and construct the landforms and
tourist sites.

SUBJECTS: Interdisciplinary: Language Arts, Social Studies, Science, Math, Technology

PRODUCT: Travelers' Aids for Interplanetary Visitors   FORMAT: Print/Display

FOCUS: Quickfacts cards to help the "traveler" in each country

LINKS:
    Language Arts:
        common phrases
        interpersonal communication
    Social Studies:
        economics
        monetary system
        cost of living
    Science:
        environmental studies
        geome characteristics
        weather patterns
        aerodynamics
    Mathematics: calculation formulas
    Technology:
        desktop publishing formats
        word processing
        graphic design

INPUT: Language Arts: cultural patterns
        vocabulary translations for various social situations
    forms of address regarding social standing
        social protocols and taboos
    Social Studies: economics
        money conversion tables
        comparison costs of similar goods and services
    Science: environmental studies
        geome characteristics: local and regional landforms, flora
          and fauna
        weather patterns: seasonal differences, major concerns
    Mathematics: calculation formulas
        principles of aerodynamics

PRODUCTS: charts, diagrams, booklets, posters, as part of final exhibition materials:
    Language Arts: booklet of handy phrases and guidelines to be used in social situations
    Social Studies: posters and charts displaying local products, prices and monetary rates
    Science: diagrams and visuals to identify likely "landing" locations and conditions for spaceship

SUBJECT: Interdisciplinary: Language Arts, Physical Education, Technology, Art, Performance

ACTIVITY: Production of Informative Booklet and Assembly Program

PRODUCT: Planning Guide

FORMAT: Written and Performance

FOCUS: Events at the Summer Olympics

CONTENT (rationale):
    1996 - 100th anniversary of modern Olympics; took place in U.S.
    high interest topic with lots of media hype and anticipation
    uses information from variety of subject areas and points of view
    demonstrates universal values of physical fitness and personal
      achievement

PROCESS (skills to be used):
    Language Arts:
        skimming and scanning of text
        notetaking and observation
        synthesis and evaluation of information from variety of
          sources
        grammar, sentence structure, and descriptive writing
    Library:
        selection of appropriate resources:
          print resources
          periodicals and newspapers
          electronic and online resources
        search strategies:
          indexes
          search engines
        comparative evaluation of resource formats and coverage

    Physical Education:
        sports basics — fitness and training
        specific events — skills and equipment

    Computer Technology:
        word processing
        elements of desktop publishing, newsletter layout
    Art:
        graphic design
        use of fonts, pictures, color
        photography (still and video) and illustrations

Performance:
>	production design
>	lighting and sound facilities
>	stage management
>	demonstration techniques and equipment

LOGISTICS:
Joint introduction of project by teachers and librarian
>	5 Olympic rings = 5 major areas of interest:
>>	1. Floor sports
>>	2. Field sports
>>	3. Water sports
>>	4. Earth sports
>>	5. Ceremonies and symbols
>	Assignment of students to committee "rings"
>	Development of timeline for all activities:
>>	Development of search strategies
>>	Research
>>	Writing and editing
>>	Paste-up and printing
>>	Performance elements
>>	Rehearsals
>>	Demonstration and distribution

INFORMATION IMPLEMENTATION:
Students will need to:
>	Identify subtopics for each "ring" of interest.
>	Formulate key questions to be answered.
>>	five key questions (subtopics) per topic
>>	minimum of five working resources per topic
>	Gather, evaluate, and organize information from both print and electronic sources.
>	Prepare short, bulleted articles for each subtopic.
>	Each student will be responsible for one subtopic, but will work cooperatively to share information and responsibility for completion of the final project with other students.

PRESENTATION: Product Formats:
Written:
>	Multi-page booklet:
>>	including masthead, table of contents, signed articles, and illustrations
>	Bibliography
>	Assembly program playbill:
>>	outline of performance schedule, performers and credits

Demonstration:
   Assembly program:
      sports demonstrations (live and video) with commentary
      displays of rings and flags
      opening and awards ceremonies
   Students will present the assembly program to the school and community and distribute the booklet to the student population in June before the actual Olympic games begin.

SUBJECT: Interdisciplinary: Social Studies, Language Arts, Math, Art

ACTIVITY: Exhibition: Architectural Adventures in the Old World

FORMAT: Written and Display
      Teachers' Activity Planning Guide

FOCUS: World History: Ancient Civilizations through Renaissance Period

CONTENT (rationale):
      culminating activity for Language Arts/ Social Studies thematic
        exploration of walls and gatekeepers; how cultures use boundaries
        to govern life
      chronological development of cultures and technologies
      mathematics units on scale, ratio, and computation
      architecture studies as historical representation of art and lifestyle
      appeal to variety of learning styles and abilities

PROCESS (skills to be used):
      Language Arts
            writing mechanics: grammar, sentence structure, and point of
               view
            narrative formats: journals and letters
            skimming and scanning of text for information
            notetaking and observation
            synthesis and evaluation of information from a variety of
               sources

      Social Studies
            identifying issues caused by geographical, cultural and
               economic changes
            techniques used for anthropological and sociological
               investigation
            analysis of maps, charts, art, and artifacts for historical data
            authority and reliability of primary sources

      Library
            topic definition:
               narrowing the target
               related topics
               concept analysis for developing search terms
            selection of appropriate resources:
               print resources and visual formats
               primary vs. secondary sources
               electronic and online resources

search strategies:
    indexes
    search engines and directories
comparative evaluation of resource formats and coverage

Mathematics
    geometric forms
    computation strategies
    estimation
    ratio and scale formulas and applications
    blueprints

Art

    form vs. function
    style and design elements
    cultural and historical influences on craft
    drawing and constructing to scale
    developing working models
    use of materials

LOGISTICS:

Coordinate all content curriculum units.
Develop project requirements, cross-content benchmarks, and rubrics for evaluation.
Identify specific architectural examples for investigation.
Develop timeline for all activities:
    Content curriculum instruction
    Instruction in research techniques
    Research time
    Progress evaluations in specific subject areas
    Final due dates for products
    "Museum" set-up and display
Introduce project to students.
Students select topics; choice of individual or team approach
Assign progress stages and due dates.

INPUT:

Location and time period of structure
Historical and political significance
Geographical, cultural, and economic significance
Format, construction, and physical size
Impact on civilization
Function as boundary:
    Wall: physical, historical, and political aspects
    Gatekeeper: personal (psychological, cultural) and
      political aspects

PRESENTATION (Product formats):

Written:

Journal entries (1-15 entries), written from choice of point of view:
Worker on construction site
Commissioner of structure
Neighbor of construction site
Anthropologist or archeologist investigating site

Architectural blueprints and diagrams, detailing
scale
materials
site layout
construction processes
cutaways

Bibliography of all resources used

Display:

Scale Model of architectural example
scale: must be no larger than 4 feet x 8 feet
able to fit through classroom doorway, and
physically carried only by project creator(s)

Information placard (8" x 11") explaining features of display

All final projects will be displayed in the commons area for grade-level exhibition, with "buildings" arranged chronologically as exhibits in a Museum of Architecture.

Instead of a "museum" display, students could design Web pages for each architectural example, with links to actual photographs and documentation available on the Web, as well as the required student-produced journals and diagrams. Web pages could be displayed in the computer lab.

Student's Project Work Guide for: Architectural Adventural Adventures in the Old World

FOCUS: (specifying)
    A. Name of structure
    B. Location, date of structure
    C. Function as Wall? Gatekeeper?

LINKS : (strategizing)
    A. Social Studies: time period
        Geographic issues
        Political/economic issues
        Cultural issues
    B. Art: history, styles
        Architecture
        Materials/crafts
    C. Math: computation formulas needed
        Graphs and diagrams
        Calculating scale and proportion
    D. Language arts:
        Readings
        Writing styles/formats

INFORMATION NEEDED: (searching, sorting, sifting, storing)
    A. Historical details
        construction rationale
        politics
        function as Wall? Gatekeeper?
    B. Art/craft:
        reason for form
        cultural impact
        style and design elements
        choice of materials
    C. Construction technology:
        blueprints and diagrams
        scale and proportion
        construction concerns and problems

PRODUCTS: (sharing)
Due On:
    A. Documents
    _____Journal
    _____Blueprints and diagrams for construction of display
    _____Bibliography: all citations

B. Display

_____Information placard

_____Structure

C. End of project observations

_____"Museum" report

_____Additional questions/topics to explore

_____Self-evaluation of:

        final products

        problem-solving processes

        production skills

SUBJECT: Extracurricular: Student Council

ACTIVITY: Planning for Fundraising Event

FORMAT: Discussion, Small Group Activity
Background:
The high school Student Council wants to stage a Renaissance Faire as a
school-wide fundraising event. Student Faire committees will be responsible
for all planning, including development of the concept, scheduling, activities,
vendors, and advertising. The faculty advisor has asked the librarian to help
students organize their preliminary research activities.

Activity Plan:
FOCUS: Strategize ways to gather information about Renaissance Faires to
develop a proposal for Board of Education approval.

LINKS:
Students:
• previous experience planning dances, programs, and country fairs
• attendance at commercially-run Renaissance Festival in nearby state
• knowledge of businesses in community that cater to or depend on teen
  patronage
• knowledge from courses in English Literature and European history

Teacher/Librarian:
• School regulations regarding requirements for student activities and fund-
  raising projects
• Available resources about Medieval and Renaissance time periods
• Search engine strategies, terminologies
• Possible Web sites, local vendors and suppliers

INPUT:
• Discuss activities at nearby festival; identify possibilities to replicate.
• Classify activities; identify categories of information needed.
        Physical space and set-up
        Historical details
        Foods
        Activities
        Vendors
        Local laws and requirements
• Discuss and identify likely resource possibilities in:
        school library
        public and university libraries (explain interlibrary loan procedures)
        business directories and yellow pages
        government and school offices
        local special interest groups
        the Internet

- Review concept analysis for design of most useful search terms, from broadest to most specific, such as:

  Fairs, festivals, and community events

  Medieval and Renaissance customs and culture,

  Historical performances and reproductions

  Art, music, crafts, food (by time period)

  Horse

  Arms and armor

  Performers and vendors

- Review use of indexes, Web access guidelines and use of online search strategies.

PAYOFFS:

- Student committees will gather information on each aspect (subtopics) of proposed Faire activity, and preparations necessary, including:

  Location/facility set-up

  Laws and local policies regarding community events

  Costumes, language and customs

  Performances and events

  Games of chance

  Vendors

  Animals

- Committees will identify local businesses and individuals as possible resources, sponsors, and additional underwriters.

- Student Council will develop event plan and proposal to submit to Board of Education for approval.

Student's Project Work Guide for: 20th Century American Literature

ACTIVITY: Pre-research Guidelines for Author Studies Project

FORMAT: Discussion and Written

Background:
Students in high school Contemporary Literature course will nominate candidates for Poet Laureate. Nominations packet for each candidate will include:
> candidate's resume´
> rationale for nomination
> list of publications
> "testimonials" from literary critics and/or other writers
> text of "acceptance speech" if chosen

Activity Plan:
FOCUS:
• Information formats to be used
• Kinds of information needed for each format

LINKS:
Students:
• Basic information about selected poet
• Forms of literary criticism
Teacher/Librarian:
• Resources available
• Broad knowledge of 20th-century literature
• Examples of business formats needed

INPUT:
• Discuss and develop nomination criteria for all candidates.
• Discuss, explain, and demonstrate purpose, layout, and scope of each format needed:
> Resumé formats — comparisons, what needs to be included, and why
> Persuasive vs. personal essays — rationale for nomination, acceptance speech
> List of publications — correct form of citations
> Testimonials — locating reviews, use of direct quotes, formats
• Review research procedures as needed

PAYOFF:
• Discuss and develop criteria for evaluating nomination packets.
• After completion of project, students will discuss and evaluate all nominations to select four finalists for the Literary Hall of Fame.

<u>Notes</u>

Chapter 4

Passing It On

As you have probably realized by now, FLIP IT! has many possible applications across the educational spectrum as well as in real life. For example, here is one teacher's outline of student responsibilities in her classroom. Class Guidelines:

Focus:

Arrive promptly; get settled quickly.

Be prepared for today's activity.

Have needed materials available and ready for use.

Logistics:

Put completed paperwork into appropriate box.

Record assignment information from blackboard.

Fulfill assigned job tasks.

Involvement:

Pay attention to directions and signals.

Lend a hand as needed.

Participate appropriately.

Clean up before leaving.

Payoffs:

Observe grading guidelines.

Earn rewards and bonuses.

Study Skills

Years ago teachers taught and students learned, or so everyone believed. Process learning skills were somehow absorbed along with the subject-specific content material as students progressed to more complex coursework. Now, however, schools recognize that many students do not intuitively learn how to learn, and as a result, a new specialization has been created. From private tutoring services to remedial courses for college students, training programs for industry, and motivational and how-to books and videos, study skills have become a major educational concern.

Study skills can be defined as "the effective use of appropriate techniques for completing a learning task...an activity that is designed to help students achieve an instructional objective." (ASCD: Tools for Learning, 1990). Most study skills fall into the following four major categories:

• Management, including:

self-motivation

organization of materials

      rules and procedures
      time management
- Information Acquisition, including:
      active listening and observing
      understanding directions
      note-taking
      information formats and text structure
      reading for meaning
      memory techniques
- Information Manipulation, including:
      selection and evaluation of data
      main ideas and subtopics
      outlining
      graphic organizers
      mnemonics, schemas, and frameworks
      remembering and reviewing
- Information Presentation, including:
      participating in discussions
      taking tests
      writing reports
      producing projects

Many of these strategies and techniques overlap in the actual applications and can be taught in a variety of ways across all the curricular strands.

Many of the teachers I have worked with now use FLIP IT! as a shorthand for the study skills strategies they teach their students to use as self-management tools.

Assignment Pad

For each homework assignment, check for the following:

    Focus: specific questions, problem? directions to be followed ? (management/acquisition)

    Load into bookbag/Lug home from locker: textbook? study sheet? other resources/materials? (management/acquisition)

    Involvement: read and respond? do problems? put together? find? (acquisition/manipulation/presentation)

    Product: work time needed? due date(s)? format? (management/manipulation/presentation)

Test Preparation

    Focus: specific topic or units covered: textbook, study sheets (management)

    Learning Cues: key words, concepts, formulas, definitions, mnemonics (acquisition/manipulation)

    Important Details: specific actions, attributes, examples (acquisition/manipulation/presentation)

Practice: chapter questions, review notes, question formats, self-quizzes, study group (management/acquisition/manipulation/presentation)

Pre/Post Unit Knowledge Webs

Focus: Identify key concepts to be covered/reviewed

Logistics:
- Have students brainstorm and web prior knowledge about the topic.
- Make master copy of group (or individual) web for each student.
- Use master web for all succeeding activities.

Information Development and Implementation:
- Have students use different colored highlighters to identify related topics.
- For each major subtopic, introduce basic concepts, and have students add to master web as information is learned.
- Again, use colored highlighters to connect related substrands.
- Have students create new subtopic webs, reorganizing and prioritizing information.

Proof:
- Hand out original master webs.
- Have students complete or redesign web, adding all material learned.
- New web can be used as a study guide for the final test, as an actual test, or as an introduction to the next unit.

How to Take Notes from Textbook

Focus: Identify the purpose or main idea of the chapter. Clues:
- title
- first and last paragraphs of chapter
- summary/questions at end of chapter

Layout: Skim to identify information markers:
- bold and/or italic print
- section/paragraph headings
- charts, pictures, diagrams

Involvement: Read one section at a time; then cover text and make notes.
- Use key words or phrases—your own words, and as few words as possible.
- Use outline or graphic organizer to categorize and organize information.
- Put "huh?" questions about information in the margins.
- Use only one side of the paper.

rePackage: Read over notes, and then restructure the information to
   show:
- key terms, ideas, and concepts
- main ideas, supporting details, and their relationships
- memory hooks: pictures, patterns, mnemonics
- summary statement

How to Construct an Essay

Focus:
- Main idea and/or crucial questions to be answered
- Key concepts, issues
- Point of view

Logistics:
- Format and terminology to be used
- Categories and patterns of information to be used
- Organization of presentation

Important Details:
- Supporting evidence
- Fact vs. opinion
- Credibility/sources of information

Presentation Requirements:
- Introductory statement
- Closing argument
- Spelling, grammar

Instructional Design

Effective instructional design requires the planner to:
- identify the focus and reasons for the activity.
- consider the links to content knowledge, strategies and applications, and students' cognitive abilities.
- structure the input and implementation required to make sure that both process and content are congruent to the objective or focus of this activity.
- assess both the product and the proof—demonstration of the students' understanding and skills mastery.

Activity Planning

(See expanded explanation in Chapter 1.)

Focus: What is the purpose of this activity?

(hint: think of Focus as **F** raming the Lesson's
   O bjectives: e.g. the
   C ontent to be delivered, the
   U tilization of this content, and the
   S trategies needed to use and understand the content.)

Logistics: What will I need to know or do in advance to make this activity
   work?

Implementation: How should I structure this activity to maximize student understanding?

Proof: How will I be able to assess student mastery of the skills/content presented at this time?

IT!: Evaluation of Intelligent Thinking: How will I be able to evaluate the success of this activity short-term and long-term?

Curriculum Development

Curriculum Development can use FLIP IT! as a framework for developing core content standards, determining articulation of subject coursework, and identifying interdisciplinary activities. Each of the four strands impact upon and overlap each other, but restructuring them this way gives a more holistic view of the curriculum, without the linear confines of traditional scope and sequence arrangements.

Focus: (internal factors)
- Unit concepts/declarative knowledge (the WHAT of this specific course)
- Unit strategies/procedural knowledge (the HOW of this specific course)
- Scheduling impacts (semester calendar, staffing, facility)

Links: (external factors)
- Foundation concepts (the WHAT of this subject discipline)
- Foundation strategies (the HOW of this subject discipline)
- School policies and schedules
- District standards and requirements
- Standardized testing concerns
- Learning styles and multiple intelligences

Input/Implementation: (delivery issues)
- Activities
- Demonstrations
- Question formats and strategies
- Scaffolding techniques
- Experiments
- Experiences
- Projects

Proof/Output: (demonstration issues)
- Knowledge
- Understanding
- Application
- Grading rubrics

Teacher Training

I offer workshops for classroom teachers to demonstrate how FLIP IT! can be used as a generic framework to:

- develop and reinforce basic study skills
- simplify classroom management techniques
- demonstrate a process to use in any problem-solving situation
- help students become independent and empowered learners
- adapt instructional techniques to meet the needs of diverse learning styles
- tie curriculum content to real-world applications
- design problem-solving activities in all curricular areas
- develop interdisciplinary and collaborative learning activities
- restructure courses of study for block scheduling
- develop rubrics for authentic assessment of student learning

At the end of these workshops, I ask teachers to complete the following grid. We start with the first column, and label it "Classroom Management." We brainstorm key words and possibilities for each of the four vertical boxes. I ask the group to reorganize themselves into three major subject areas (e.g., Social Studies and Language Arts, Science and Math, Art and Music) and work together to fill in the next column for their own kinds of applications. Then we round-robin the worksheets, until each group has filled in a column on every paper. As we compare notes, we discover that FLIP IT! works across all curriculum areas and all kinds of problem solving situations.

FLIP IT! for effective problem solving
WE'RE ALL SPEAKING THE SAME LANGUAGE

FOCUS					
LINKS					
INPUT					
PAYOFF					

Figure 4.1

According to the SCANS Report (1991), essential skills for the workplace of the 21st century include:

- decision making
- creative thinking
- ability to conceptualize and imagine
- knowing how to learn
- reasoning
- problem solving

No matter what fancy name we give these sets of skills:

- Problem-Based Learning Techniques
- Lifetime Learning Strategies for Tomorrow's Taxpayers
- Information Navigation Aptitudes and Attitudes, or even
- Patterns and Paradigms for Effective Educational Activities

they are still information literacy skills, using metacognitive (thinking about thinking) concepts and a constructivist (building on what students already know) approach to help students learn how to use information independently and successfully.

If the purpose of all education is to prepare students to be

- goal-oriented
- purposeful and productive
- strategic and self-evaluative

citizens, then using FLIP IT! as both framework and mnemonic can be a simple, effective way to help students learn how to be active learners, thinkers, and problem solvers, so that they will become effective information consumers and producers.

<u>Notes</u>

Got a problem to solve?

FLIP IT!

Focus:
Stop and think! Identify specifics.

Link:
What do you already know?

Input:
Implement the Information you find.

Payoff:
Put it all together

for

Intelligent Thinking!

Reproducible from *FLIP IT! An Information Skills Strategy for Student Researchers* by Alice H. Yucht (1997, Linworth Publishing, Inc.)

Formula for Effective Information Problem Solving

FOCUS

X

(LINKS + INPUT)

$$\overline{\overline{}}$$

PAYOFF

Reproducible from *FLIP IT! An Information Skills Strategy for Student Researchers* by Alice H. Yucht (1997, Linworth Publishing, Inc.)

FOCUS FRAMES:
ZOOMING IN ON THE SUBJECT

DIRECTIONS:

1. Brainstorm and write down possible subtopics and questions about your topic in the big frame.

2. Identify the related topics within the big frame.

3. Re-organize (group and rewrite) these subtopics into the small frames.

4. Write useful key words/search terms for each subtopic on the lines next to the small frames.

SUB-TOPIC:

SUB-TOPIC:

SUB-TOPIC:

SUB-TOPIC:

PATHFINDER GUIDE FOR RESEARCH ON:

_____

search terms (key words) to use:

_____ _____ _____ _____ _____

_____ _____ _____ _____ _____

suggested resources: **call numbers / location:**

A. BASIC INFORMATION AND OVERVIEW:

    General encyclopedias: _____

    Special encylopedias: _____

    Dictionaries: _____

    Almanacs: _____

    Atlas: _____

B. MORE DETAILED INFORMATION:

    Books about subject: _____

    Books about related subjects: _____

    Multi-media formats, including CD-ROMs: _____

    Online databases: _____

C. INFORMATION ABOUT RECENT EVENTS:

    Readers' Guide to Periodical Literature: _____

    Magazine Article Summaries: _____

ADDITIONAL RESOURCES: **source:**

    Internet sites: _____

    Broadcasts (radio/television):   _____

    Community Resources: _____

    Personal interviews: _____

CITATIONS of RESOURCES USED
Multi-volume Resource (encyclopedias, etc.)

_____
sub-topic

_____,_____ . " _____ .
Author's name (if given): last name first.   **Title of article (in quotation marks).**

_____ . _____,_____ .
Name of encyclopedia (underlined).   **Publishing company, copyright date.**

_____,_____ .
volume, page(s).

_____
sub-topic

_____,_____ . " _____ .
Author's name (if given): last name first.   **Title of article (in quotation marks).**

_____ . _____,_____ .
Name of encyclopedia (underlined).   **Publishing company, copyright date.**

_____,_____ .
volume, page(s).

_____
sub-topic

_____,_____ . " _____ .
Author's name (if given): last name first.   **Title of article (in quotation marks).**

_____ . _____,_____ .
Name of encyclopedia (underlined).   **Publishing company, copyright date.**

_____,_____ .
volume, page(s).

_____
sub-topic

_____,_____ . " _____ .
Author's name (if given): last name first.   **Title of article (in quotation marks).**

_____ . _____,_____ .
Name of encyclopedia (underlined).   **Publishing company, copyright date.**

_____,_____ .
volume, page(s).

FLIP IT! 4-BOX note-taking format

Research topic:_____   **Researcher's name:**_____

FOCUS:
Questions/Key Words

A.

B.

C.

D.

E.

LOOKED UP IN:
List of resources used:

*

+

$

@

IMPORTANT POINTS:
Facts I found

1.

2.

3.

4.

5.

6.

7.

8.

9.

10.

Reproducible from *FLIP IT! An Information Skills Strategy for Student Researchers* by Alice H. Yucht (1997, Linworth Publishing, Inc.)

Give credit where it's due

 Cite (give publishing information about)

the

 Site (the resource you used)

where you

 Sighted (located, took notes about)

your facts.

Reproducible from *FLIP IT! An Information Skills Strategy for Student Researchers* by Alice H. Yucht (1997, Linworth Publishing, Inc.)

LIBRARY ACTIVITY PLANNING GUIDE

Teacher: _____ Subject: _____ date: _____

FOCUS: (specifying)
Students will be investigating:
> **TOPIC(s):**
>> **as part of Unit of Study on:**
>
> **Rationale:**

LINKS/LOGISTICS: (strategizing)
A. Prior knowledge/skills students should have:
> **Content:**
> **Process:**

B. Resources:
> **Recommendations:**
> **Restrictions:**

C. Constraints: e.g. time, facilities, student abilities

INPUT/IMPLEMENTATION: (searching, sorting, sifting, storing)
Content:
> **Kinds of information needed:**

Process:
> **Library/Information Skills:**
> **Thinking/Writing Activities:**

PRODUCT/PROOF: (sharing)
Product Format: **Product Requirements:**

Assignment timeline: DATES:

Introduction:	_____ in class	_____ in library	
Library Work:	_____ search strategies	_____ notetaking	
Due Dates:	_____ notes	_____ work in progress	
		_____ related activities	
	_____ bibliography	_____ final product	

Reproducible from *FLIP IT! An Information Skills Strategy for Student Researchers* by Alice H. Yucht (1997, Linworth Publishing, Inc.)

FLIPS IT! for effective problem solving
WE'RE ALL SPEAKING THE SAME LANGUAGE

FOCUS				
LINKS				
INPUT				
PAYOFF				

New Jersey Core Curriculum
Content Standards

Introduction

At the threshold to the twenty-first century, New Jersey finds itself struggling along with the rest of the nation to educate citizens who will be competitive in the international market-place of the future. New Jersey also faces a particular constitutional challenge of implementing a state system of "Thorough and Efficient" public schools.

New Jersey wrestles with a paradox regarding the governance of public education. Ours is a state with a 120-year-old constitutional guarantee that regardless of residency, its children will receive a "Thorough and Efficient" education. Throughout this same time period, the State has evolved into approximately 600 independent school districts that exercise considerable "local control." Confronting the State, therefore, is the issue of how to ensure that all children receive a "T&E;" education. This challenge is exacerbated by the fact that each district determines its own curriculum.

Core curriculum content standards are an attempt to define the meaning of "Thorough" in the context of the 1875 State constitutional guarantee that students would be educated within a Thorough and Efficient system of free public schools. They describe what all students should know and be able to do upon completion of a thirteen-year public education.

These standards are not meant to serve as a statewide curriculum guide. They define the results expected but do not limit district strategies for how to ensure that their students achieve these expectations. To assist local educators, the standards will be further elaborated through curriculum frameworks. While also not a curriculum, these frameworks will bring to life the intent of the standards through classroom examples and a discussion of the underlying rationales. Local curriculum developers can use the frameworks as a resource to develop district curricula that best meet the needs of the students in each community. Curriculum frameworks also serve as a resource to classroom teachers and to staff developers who want to modify instruction in light of the new standards.

Since our schools need to produce both excellent thinkers and excellent doers, the core curriculum content standards describe what students should know and be able to do in specific academic areas and across disciplines. Content standards are concerned with the knowledge students should acquire and the skills they should develop in the course of their K-12 experience. That is why each of the content standards is further described in terms of cumulative progress indicators at specific benchmark grades of 4, 8, and 12. Over the next few years, the content standards will be further defined through the attachment of performance tasks and levels which will be determined as the standards are integrated into the state assessment program.

These standards will directly influence the new grade four test and the current state assessment program at grade 8 (Early Warning Test) and at grade 11 (High School Proficiency Test). In future years, the core curriculum standards will define the State's high school graduation requirements. In their broadest application, these standards will establish the foundation upon which students can build as they pursue further learning and careers.

The standards emerged from the efforts of two different groups that worked one after another for a total of fifteen months in 1992-93 and 1995. In 1992-93, panels of educators, business people and other citizens developed preliminary draft standards in seven academic areas and career education. During 1995, similarly constituted working groups built upon these preliminary standards and engaged the public in a review process that resulted in several revised drafts.

The 1995 working groups submitted a total of 85 standards comprised of 1195 indicators to the Department of Education. The department reviewed the standards proposed for eight content areas and extracted the following five cross-content workplace readiness standards which apply to all areas of instruction:

1. All students will develop career planning and workplace readiness skills.
2. All students will use technology, information, and other tools.
3. All students will use critical thinking, decision-making, and problem-solving skills.
4. All students will demonstrate self-management skills.

Reprinted by permission of the New Jersey Department of Education

5. All students will apply safety principles.

Through these five cross-content workplace readiness standards, the knowledge and skills associated with career education have been elevated in importance for all instructional areas. As a pilot state for the federal "School-to-Work" initiative, New Jersey emphasizes the importance of every student linking school-based learning with a career major and of having both school-based and work-based learning experiences. Since one of the goals of public education is to prepare students for the world of work, it is important that these standards be addressed through all content areas.

The department also emphasized the essential results expected for students by distilling the working groups' recommendations into 56 standards covering the following seven academic content areas:

- Visual and Performing Arts
- Comprehensive Health and Physical Education
- Language Arts/Literacy
- Mathematics
- Science
- Social Studies
- World Languages

The humanities, which explore the human condition, have been integrated throughout the discrete academic content areas. They have not been treated as a separate content area because they are by definition interdisciplinary. Likewise, several other specific curriculum areas have not been designated as separate components of the core curriculum. These include family and consumer science, technology education, business education and other occupational areas. However, these content areas can contribute to students' achieving the expected results set forth in the standards, especially the cross-content workplace readiness standards. In addition, these programs provide students with opportunities to apply, and thereby reinforce, learning from the core curriculum content areas.

While the standards areas include concepts that can be measured in a uniform manner, they do not include the affective domain, which addresses areas of self-esteem, emotions, feelings, and personal values. Certainly, students' intellectual growth is affected by their emotional disposition. However, the Department of Education excluded desirable affective results from the content standards which the State would formally assess, because it would be inappropriate for the State to make judgments about student values or feelings. The department's position is that parents and local educators should make judgments about when and how these affective issues will be addressed in their communities. Teachers, administrators, parents, and other community residents all have a responsibility to nurture and communicate the values, self-worth, and character development required for young people to succeed.

Although the standards have been organized into seven separate academic areas and five cross-content workplace readiness standards, this is not meant to imply that each standard can be met only through courses in a formal school setting. The application of knowledge from all content areas can be reinforced through experiences beyond the school walls, such as volunteer activities, job shadowing, and part-time jobs.

Other parts of the educational system and the larger community can be used to deliver an integrated curriculum. For example, career education should be incorporated into all seven content areas as well as into occupational education programs. Language arts and literacy skills are key to success in all areas of learning. Science is an important part of health education and represents an important part of the historical record. Mathematics skills are tools for problem-solving in science and can be reinforced in vocational-technical areas. Technology education teachers can show the application of problem-solving techniques which bring physics principles to life. Family and consumer sciences (home economics) draws on health and science in preparing students for family living. The visual and performing arts provide an avenue for the understanding of science, social studies, language arts, world languages, and design technology.

In one sense, these core curriculum content standards mark with precision the results expected of all students. In another sense, they serve as a banner behind which all segments of the education community and the state at large can mobilize to reshape our approach to education. Collectively, they embody a vision of the skills and understandings all of New Jersey's children need to step forward into the twenty-first century and to be successful in their careers and daily lives.

Cross-Content Workplace Readiness Standards

Introduction

As the content committees met and reviewed the eight subject specific standards (the seven listed areas plus career education), certain themes reoccurred. These common themes reinforce the notion that each content area draws on key elements of other content areas. For example, the need for students to learn problem-solving and critical thinking skills was reflected in all of the sets of standards. Since these cross-content workplace readiness standards are important to the success of all students in all content areas, they have been identified here for special emphasis:

1. All students will develop career planning and workplace readiness skills.
2. All students will use technology, information and other tools.
3. All students will use critical thinking, decision-making, and problem-solving skills.
4. All students will demonstrate self-management skills.
5. All students will apply safety principles.

While the indicators for the cross-content workplace readiness standards are not broken out by grade level, districts should begin building these concepts into their programs at the K-4 level in age appropriate activities, e.g., focusing on positive work habits. Other of the concepts are more appropriate for the higher grade levels, e.g., preparing a resume and completing job applications. The following is a list of the cross-content workplace readiness standards, with cumulative progress indicators of student skills in each area. Unlike the progress indicators for the seven specific content sections, these indicators are not broken down into grade level clusters because, in addition to crossing all content areas, they also cross all grade levels. Teachers should integrate these concepts into all programs in content-specific and grade-appropriate ways.

Similar concepts have also been identified by members of the business and industry communities as vital. In a 1992 national report, the Secretary's Commission on Achieving Necessary Skills (SCANS) identified several of these concepts as necessary for success in the world of work. The following chart lists the SCANS Workplace Competencies and Foundation Skills referenced with the cross-content workplace readiness standards.

SCANS And Cross-Content Workplace Readiness Standards

Standard 3:
All Students Will Use Critical Thinking, Decision Making and Problem-Solving Skills

Descriptive Statement: Students will be expected to develop original thoughts and ideas, think creatively, develop habits of inquiry, and take intellectual and performance risks. They will be expected to recognize problems, devise a variety of ways to solve these problems, analyze the potential advantages and disadvantages of each alternative, and evaluate the effectiveness of the method ultimately selected.

Cumulative Progress Indicators

All students will be able to:
1. Recognize and define a problem, or clarify decisions to be made.
2. Use models, relationships, and observations to clarify problems and potential solutions.
3. Formulate questions and hypotheses.
4. Identify and access resources, sources of information, and services in the school and the community.
5. Use the library media center as a critical resource for inquiry and assessment of print and nonprint materials.
6. Plan experiments.
7. Conduct systematic observations.
8. Organize, synthesize, and evaluate information for appropriateness and completeness.
9. Identify patterns and investigate relationships.
10. Monitor and validate their own thinking.
11. Identify and evaluate the validity of alternative solutions.

12. Interpret and analyze data to draw conclusions.
13. Select and apply appropriate solutions to problem-solving and decision-making situations.
14. Evaluate the effectiveness of various solutions.
15. Apply problem-solving skills to original and creative/design projects.

SCANS Workplace Competencies

Effective workers can productively use:	*Cross-Content Standards*
Resources — They know how to allocate time, money, materials, space, and staff.	Demonstrate self-management skills.
Interpersonal skills — They can work on teams, teach others, serve customers, lead, negotiate, and work well with people from culturally diverse backgrounds.	Demonstrate self-management skills. Develop career planning and workplace readiness skills.
Information —They can acquire and evaluate data, organize and maintain files, interpret and communicate, and use computers to process information.	Use technology, information and other tools.
Systems — They understand social, organizational, and technological systems; they can monitor and correct performance; and they can design or improve systems.	Use technology, information and other tools.
Technology — They can select equipment and tools, apply technology to specific tasks, and maintain and troubleshoot equipment.	Use technology, information and other tools.

SCANS Foundations Skills

Competent workers in the high-performance workplace need:	*Cross-Content Standards*
Basic Skills — reading, writing, arithmetic and mathematics, speaking and listening.	The seven sections of core content standards address this area.
Thinking Skills — the ability to learn, to reason, to think creatively, to make decisions, and to solve problems.	Use critical thinking, decision-making, and problem-solving skills.
Personal Qualities — individual responsibility, self-esteem and self-management, sociability, integrity, and honesty.	Demonstrate self-management skills. Apply safety principles.

Bibliography

AASL/AECT. *Information Power; guidelines for School Library Media Programs*. American Library Association, 1988.

AASL/AECT National Guidelines Vision Committee. *Information Literacy Standards for Student Learning* (draft). [Online] Available at http://www.ala.org/aasl/infopwrmenu.html.

Baker, J. & A. *From Puzzles to Projects: Solving Problems All the Way*. Heinemann, 1993.

Black, Howard & Sandra. *Organizing Thinking: Graphic Organizers*. Critical Thinking Press, 1990.

Bleakley, Ann and Jackie L. Carrigan. *Resource-based Learning Activities: Information Literacy for High School Students*. American Library Association, 1994.

Brady, Marion. *What's Worth Teaching? Selecting, Organizing, and Integrating Knowledge*. SUNY Press, 1989.

Breivik, Patricia Senn. *Information Literacy: Educating Children for the 21st Century*. Scholastic, 1994.

Brooks, Jacqueline Grennon. *In Search of Understanding: The Case for Constructivist Classrooms*. Association for Supervision and Curriculum Development, 1993.

California Media and Library Educators Association. *From Library Skills to Information Literacy: A Handbook for the 21st century*. Hi Willow, 1994.

Christen, William L. *The A.T.L.A.S.S. program: The Application and Teaching of Learning and Study Skills*. Kendall/Hunt, 1987.

Clark, Edward T. *Designing and Implementing an Integrated Curriculum: A Student-centered Approach*. Holistic Education Press, 1997.

Clarke, John H. *Patterns of Thinking: Integrating Learning Skills in Content Teaching*. Allyn & Bacon, 1990.

Cleaver, Betty P. and William D. Taylor. *The Instructional Consultant Role of the School Library Media Specialist*. American Library Association, 1989.

Costa, Arthur L. and Lawrence F. Lowery. *Techniques for Teaching Thinking*. Critical Thinking Press, 1989.

Eisenberg, Michael B. and Robert E. Berkowitz. *Information Problem-solving: The Big Six Skills Approach to Library & Information Skills Instruction.* Ablex, 1990.

Farmer, Lesley S. J. *Cooperative Learning Activities in the Library Media Center.* Libraries Unlimited, 1991.

Farmer, Lesley S. J. *Creative Partnerships: Librarians and Teachers Working Together.* Linworth Publishing, 1993.

Farmer, Lesley, S. J. *Workshops for Teachers: Becoming Partners for Information Literacy.* Linworth Publishing, 1995.

Gail, M.D. et al. *Tools for Learning: A Guide to Teaching Study Skills.* Association for Supervision and Curriculum Development, 1990.

Gaskins, Irene, and Thorne Elliot. *Implementing Cognitive Strategy Instruction Across the School: The Benchmark Manual for Teachers.* Brookline Books, 1991.

Haycock, Ken. *Program Advocacy: Power, Publicity, and the Teacher-librarian.* Libraries Unlimited, 1990.

Harmin, Merrill. *Inspiring Active Learners: A Handbook for Teachers.* Association for Supervision and Curriculum Development, 1994.

Hunkins, Francis P. *Teaching Thinking Through Effective Questioning.* Christopher-Gordon, 1989.

Jones, B. F., et al. *Strategic Teaching and Learning: Cognitive Instruction in the Content Areas.* Association for Supervision and Curriculum Development, 1987.

Karelse, Cathy-Mae and Peter G. Underwood. *Travelling the Superhighway.* [Online] Available at http://www.inc.co.za/online/hero/may_5/trav.html.

Karelse, Cathy-Mae and Peter G. Underwood. *Seeking Answers on the Superhighway.* [Online] Available at http://www.inc.co.za/online/hero/may_12/super.html.

Karelse, Cathy-Mae and Peter G. Underwood. *Alternative Routes on the Superhighway.* [Online] Available at http://www.inc.co.za/online/hero/may_19/hiway3.html.

Kirby, Dan and Carol Kuykendall. *Mind Matters: Teaching for Thinking.* Boynton/Cook, 1991.

Kovalik, Susan. *ITI: The Model: Integrated Thematic Instruction.* Books for Educators,1994.

Kuhlthau, Carol C. *Implementing a Process Approach to Information Skills: A Study Identifying Indicators of Success in Library Media Programs.* [Online] Available at http://copper.ucs.indiana.edu/~callison/kuhlthau/ kuhlthau.html.

Kuhlthau, Carol C. *Teaching the Library Research Process: A Step-by-Step Program for Secondary School Students.* Center for Applied Research in Education, 1985.

Langrehr, J. *Teaching Students to Think.* National Educational Service, 1988.

Marzano, R. J. *A Different Kind of Classroom: Teaching with Dimensions of Learning.* Association for Supervision and Curriculum Development, 1992.

Marzano, R. J., et al. *Dimensions of Thinking: A Framework for Curriculum and Instruction.* Association for Supervision and Curriculum Development, 1988.

Minnesota Educational Media Organization. *Information Connections: Guidelines for Minnesota School Media Programs.* MEMO, 1992.

New Jersey Department of Education. *Core Curriculum Content Standards.* NJDOE, 1996.

Pitts, Judy M. *Personal Understanding and Mental Models of Information.* Dissertation, Florida State University, 1994.

Rafoth, Mary Ann, et al. *Strategies for Learning and Remembering: Study Skills Across the Curriculum.* National Education Association, 1993.

Robinson, Adam. *What Smart Students Know: Maximum Grades, Optimum Learning, Minimum Time.* Random House, 1993.

Secretary's Commission on Achieving Necessary Skills. What Work Requires of Schools: A SCANS Report for America 2000. U S Department of Labor, 1991.

Skapura, Robert. *Seven Steps to Successful Term Papers.* Workshop presentations, 1987-90.

Stripling, Barbara K., and Judy M. Pitts. *Brainstorms and Blueprints: Teaching Library Research as a Thinking Process.* Libraries Unlimited, 1988.

Swartz, Robert J. and D.N. Perkins. *Teaching Thinking: Issues & Approaches*. Critical Thinking Press, 1990.

Turner, Philip M. *Helping Teachers Teach*. Libraries Unlimited, 1985.

Weisburg, Hilda K., and Ruth Toor. *Learning, Linking & Critical Thinking: Information Strategies for the K-12 Library Media Curriculum*. Library Learning Resources, Inc., 1994.